Whom God Has Joined

SKETCHES FROM A MARRIAGE IN WHICH GOD IS FIRST

ISOBEL KUHN

EDITED BY M. E. TEWKSBURY

OMF BOOKS

Copyright © 2004, OMF International

Published by OMF International.
10 West Dry Creek Circle, Littleton CO 80120

ISBN : 978-1-929122-01-1

First published *2001*
This printing *2013*

All rights reserved, including translation. No part of this book may be reproduced or transmitted in any form or by any means, electronic or mechanical, including photocopying, recording, or any information storage and retrieval system without written permission from OMF International, 2 Cluny Road, Singapore 259570, Republic of Singapore. Printed in the United States of America.

Portions of this book appeared in *One Vision Only*, Carolyn Canfield, copyright © 1959 OMF International.

OMF BOOKS

OMF Books are distributed worldwide.
Visit *www.OMFBooks.com* for more information.

CONTENTS

Chapter 1	Anticipation	7
Chapter 2	Getting Married is Not a Private Affair After All	11
Chapter 3	What Comes First?	17
Chapter 4	How to Develop a Taste for Bean Curd	23
Chapter 5	His Wonderful Cook—As Viewed by Her	31
Chapter 6	Speech Seasoned with Salt	41
Chapter 7	John Becomes "Daddy"	47
Chapter 8	Counting Raindrops	54
Chapter 9	Unwanted Assignment	59
Chapter 10	Beginnings at Yungping	63
Chapter 11	The Forgotten Cloak	71
Chapter 12	A Hard Day	75
Chapter 13	A Glimpse of Storybook Land	81
Chapter 14	A Parting That Did Not Part	89
Chapter 15	The Thing With the Stuff in It	95
Chapter 16	Furlough Without Baggage (1936)	99
Chapter 17	Working the Thing That is Good	103
Chapter 18	Home Town	107
Chapter 19	The Ticklish Question	113
What Happened After		121

CHAPTER ONE
Anticipation

WE MET IN THE KITCHEN of the Moody Bible Institute (MBI) in Chicago, in the year 1924. We were both students working our way through school. He had the job of running the dish-washing machine. At that important moment, I was in the line of waitresses, waiting for the hot food we would carry to the tables. It was just one minute before the bell that would set us all in motion.

I was a new student, impatient to get through my training so that I might be God's messenger to the Lisu tribe of the China-Burma border. As I waited, I dreamed of that mountain land. *Two years more of this before I can get there!* I thought disconsolately.

The dishwasher had also gone into a daydream as he waited for the bell to ring. One foot up on a chair, chin in hand, he dreamed out into space, unconscious that he was facing the line of waitresses. As I turned quickly, I found myself suddenly falling down into the well of two blue eyes. Down, down I went until soul met soul and the shock brought us to. Quickly each turned away and tried to get busy with something else, but it had happened.

I did not even know his name. It was three months before we were formally introduced, yet every day I had to pass him in order to put away dishes. We never looked at each other or spoke, yet somehow I was perfectly sure that Blue Eyes had investigated me, that he knew my name and all about me! I was right.

I was slower to find out about him. He had come two semesters before and knew how to make subtle inquiries. Eventually I learned he was John Kuhn, although his name didn't matter. From that first moment on, *HE* was capitalized and italicized in my thinking.

Somewhat later I discovered we were both volunteers for China and both interested in the China Inland Mission (CIM). The formal introduction took place on Clark Street one evening, where we gathered to go to a surprise party for Dr. Isaac Page. From then on, it was proper to converse when we met in the MBI kitchen. The first request for a date took place while I was filling the evening teapot at the hot water urn!

The CIM prefers that engagements take place after candidates are both accepted. That way, if one must be turned down, for medical or other reasons, both are not lost to the missionary cause. For this reason, Dr. Page, a representative of the CIM and an intimate friend of my father's, was stern in his warnings about budding friendships. We were obedient. John graduated and sailed for China in the fall of 1926. There was not even an understanding between us.

The next term, in December of 1926, I graduated. By the time I attended the CIM's candidate school in Toronto, the foreign uprisings of 1927 had begun in China and the CIM was not able to send out any new workers for nearly two years. That is why John got to China two years before I did.

After I was accepted by the China Inland Mission, John Kuhn's letters began to have a personal note which meant only one thing. But I was still uncertain. I felt called to the Lisu tribe of Yunnan province. John had been somewhat interested in the far northwest of Kansu—the opposite direction.

I wrote John's sister, Kathryn Kuhn Harrison, telling her to warn him not to propose until he had been designated. My letter crossed with one of his. Designations had taken place earlier than expected and he was assigned to the tribes of Yunnan! Would I be his wife and go with him? He asked me to cable the answer: "light" if I accepted him, "dark" if I refused.

There was no question in my mind as to what my answer was, yet as I spread that precious letter out before the Lord there was still a problem. John and I are of very opposite dispositions, each rather strong minded. Science has never discovered what happens when the irresistible force collides with the immovable object. Whatever would happen if they married one another? "Lord, it must occur sooner or later. Are You sufficient for even that?"

The verse the Lord gave me was Matthew 6:33, "Seek ye first the kingdom of God, and His righteousness; and all these things shall be added unto you." I cabled back "light," then wrote a letter suggesting that our marriage motto be "God first."

The cable was directed to Shanghai Headquarters, but John was living in a house some distance away and had to be sent for. When he read the word "light" he was so transported with joy that, getting on the street car to return home, he dreamily sailed right past the conductor, forgetting the small earthly matter of paying his fare! The conductor, being well rooted in the earth, gave a grunt and followed him in pursuit. The grins of fellow travelers brought John somewhat to his senses!

WE WERE TO BE MARRIED in Kunming, the capital of Yunnan province. John was stationed down the railway line at a little town named Chengchiang. I was studying language in Kunming. We had planned on November 14, 1929 for our wedding day, but suddenly had to change it to November 4. The American Consul had an unexpected call to leave the city and could not be present if we kept the later date.

Hastily, I sent a runner to Chengchiang to ask if John could make the earlier day. He brought the answer himself! Our tongues flew as we discussed new arrangements—until the ring was mentioned. "Oh," cried my bridegroom, "didn't I go and forget the wedding ring! I left it in a box in Chengchiang!" Well, in such a big city, we would be able to borrow a substitute, and we were not superstitious, so it was all right.

But even that oversight was corrected. Chu Yin-chang, the young Chinese who was John's cook, companion, and "boy" arrived the next day, the wedding ring with him! After John left, Yin-chang had been going through his drawers and found the little box. Knowing what it was, he had brought it along. John had always been loud in the praises of his wonderful cook; now the encomiums soared sky high. It never occurred to either of us to ask what he was doing going through his master's bureau drawers. The world was all rosy and everyone in it a contributor to our joy.

That evening we went for a walk outside the city gate where there were stretches of rice fields and not many pedestrians. "Just think, dear," I said, beaming, "this time next week we will be married!"

"Ye-es," answered my dearly beloved, but in such a gloomy voice that I cast him a startled look. "Yes, we will have been married. And then there will be nothing to look forward to!"

Anticipation! It had tasted so sweet he was reluctant to see it slip away!

Chapter Two
Getting Married is Not a Private Affair After All

THE CHINA INLAND MISSION had two houses in Kunming, provincial capital of Yunnan. One was the guest house and business center which served all our missionaries in the province. The other was the home of the missionary couple who supervised the work in the local church and on the many outstations established in country towns around the city. John was staying at the guest house, I was with the church workers, and the hostess at each place took a keen interest in our wedding. Let us call them Mrs. A and Mrs. B.

Mrs. A was the ascetic type who felt that missionaries should live with the nationals and be as self-denying as possible. Mrs. B, who was in charge of the guest house, had a distinct gift for arranging her home in an attractive style and did not feel it wrong to spend a little money to maintain it. Since many of our Yunnan workers lived in the mountains among the tribes where life was primitive and hard, she felt that on the few occasions which brought them out to civilization for medical or dental treatment, they should have comfortable rooms and good food. Obviously, two such opposite dispositions would not always agree.

My own idea of a wedding was of an occasion so sacred that we would not wish to have many onlookers. By nature I am the solitaire who does not enjoy crowds. John was my opposite in this. To him, the more people around, the more joy it gave him. However, men are usually shy on their wedding day, and he was with me in wanting only a few people present when we exchanged our vows before the Lord.

It was customary for the hostess at the guest house to assume the responsibility of entertainment in place of the bride's mother, so we proceeded to confide in Mrs. B our wish that only a select few be present.

Now in some of these Far Eastern countries, the white community does not often have reason for a celebration together, so a wedding is regarded as a social affair. I had noted a peculiar expression pass over Mrs. B's face when I first intimated that we did not wish a crowd at our wedding, but she kindly repressed her own sentiments and left me none the wiser.

Shopping one day, however, I was stopped by a lady of another mission. She was a sympathetic, motherly soul and gave my hand a warm squeeze. "My dear," she said, "I hear that you are to be married! Well, I just love weddings. You won't mind if I just slip into the back seat and look on, will you? I don't want anything to eat, you understand!" This last was added hurriedly, much to my amusement. It was obvious now that she was thinking our plans for such a small affair might have a financial reason.

I could not be blunt and say, "It's because I don't want half-strangers at such a sacred moment." There was nothing to do but to invite warm-hearted Mrs. X to come. So I asked Mrs. B to prepare for one more. Again there came that quizzical smile, but nothing was said, and I went blissfully on.

The next day another lady stopped me on the street and asked to come in on that back bench at our wedding! She was also profuse in her assurance that she did not need anything to eat! I invited her, too. What else could one do?

When I reported this to Mrs. B she looked anxious. "Miss Miller," she said, "I do not see how you can possibly invite Mrs. X and Mrs. Z and leave out Mrs. Y. Mrs. Y is an old friend of the mission. She would never dream of giving a wedding and not inviting me, for instance. And Mrs. X is a comparative newcomer. And if Mrs. W heard that X, Y, and Z were invited and she left out! Dear me, I am sorry, but I do not know where you are going to draw the line. I do hope this wedding of yours will not cause ill feelings."

After the wedding we would be going to our station and would seldom see these people again, but Mrs. B must continue to live among them. We saw the point and, to cut a long story short, we ended up with the inevitable—all the westerners of Kunming were invited.

This was not the end of our problems. One evening, some days before the wedding, my hostess Mrs. A appeared at the supper table looking rather fatigued but triumphant. "I've been all day working over at the Peng Gardens, getting some rooms ready for you and John to occupy for your honeymoon," she announced. "There is no reason why you should spend money going across the lake, when the CIM still has a lease on that place. You have Yin-chang and his bride to cook for you, and you will have a lovely time right among the Chinese."

It sounded reasonable and I was quite overwhelmed with her kindness in laboring so for us. I was not slow to tell Mrs. B of this unexpected graciousness. But I was quite unprepared for Mrs. B's reaction.

"Oh, but you can't do that!" she almost wailed. "I've arranged for you to rent the honeymoon cottage across the lake. It does not cost much for a week. I meant to send your meals over to you by boat, so you would be quite alone with all those lovely walks and the climb to the temple and the Chinese village to visit. Peng's Gardens? And Yin-chang to cook for you! Why, he and his wife would watch everything you did—with the Peng family to aid them. A honeymoon comes only once in a lifetime. Oh, I do hope you won't feel you have to accept just because Mrs. A spent a morning cleaning the place up!"

It was easy to see that Mrs. B was distressed over the matter. At the same time, Mrs. A was quite taking it for granted that we were going to Peng Gardens, and telling people so. John and I retired for consultation.

"Well, let's go to Peng Gardens," John said, "Since Mrs. A has gone to such trouble. And it is true we would have Yin-chang to do the cooking for us."

"But Mrs. B has brought out a point that we were too inexperienced to foresee for ourselves," I replied thoughtfully. "If I remember rightly, you yourself have been telling me that in Chinese eyes, the chaste and high-minded newlyweds observe the greatest indifference to one another in public. They are never seen to speak to one another until the first child is born. Didn't you say that? And they never call each other by their first names. The bride refers to him as the person outside the house and the groom refers to her as the person inside the house. When we begin to live among the Chinese we must be careful to conform to their ideas in this manner. But I certainly hope I can have at least one week when I may treat you and be treated normally. Just think how curious the Pengs and Yin-chang would be; we would be watched every moment."

"Well, that is true. So then we'd better decide to go across the lake, eh?"

"That would be ideal, as Mrs. B advised. But seeing that feeling is running rather warm between the two as to whose advice we are to take, I think the most important matter is not where to go, but how we can avoid resentment between Mrs. A and Mrs. B over the matter. After all, we will be leaving here and seldom returning. But they must continue to live just around the corner from one another ad infinitum. I would prefer that they both be disgusted with us, rather than that anything resembling a root of bitterness spring up between them. Is it necessary to have a honeymoon at all? Can we not go right off to our station?"

"No, we can't do that. There's no night train. We've got to spend our wedding night somewhere near here. There's no town where we get off the train and no place to hire coolies for our luggage and your mountain chair. I've already arranged for coolies to come over the mountain from Chengchiang to meet our train on that day. We have to make that connection or we'll be in a pickle for sure."

"Well, what can we do?" We thought and thought.

"Is there no third place we can go for a honeymoon, dear?" I asked at length. "You've been here for other weddings."

"Yes," John said. "Most missionaries go across the lake to that cottage Mrs. B is talking about. But there is a French hotel, you know. Business people sometimes go there, I believe. But my, that costs!"

The French hotel was run on European lines by a European manager and mainly catered to the French population of Kunming. Being officials in the Salt Gabelle or other industries, they were usually well-to-do people.

The arrival of mail from America brought a deciding factor. There was a letter from John's father in which he enclosed a substantial check as a wedding gift for us!

"Here we are, Belle!" John cried, grinning and waving that important piece of slim paper. "Here is enough for a week's honeymoon at the French hotel!"

"Good," I answered. "Dear Daddy Kuhn, bless his

heart! Mrs. B will be as horrified at our extravagance as Mrs. A. But it is not misusing any money given for mission purposes. It has absolutely no tags on it. We'll let Daddy Kuhn give us our honeymoon." And so it was settled.

The news of our decision caused both Mrs. A and Mrs. B to throw up their hands in dismay, as we had foreseen. This unexpected unity of opinion paved the way for them to do the best they could for such reckless youngsters who had yet to learn CIM economies.

I always thought that our wedding was the most beautiful of any I had ever seen. We were married in the Chinese church, and the good ladies had transformed it. The whole looked like a lawn party in the woods! It was a completely happy day.

As we rode off in rickshas for the French hotel, we turned to wave to our group of friends. There were our two dear hostesses, standing in unconscious union, trying to wave hopefully to us, but each dubiously shaking her head over those unmanageable and extravagant Kuhns!

Chapter Three
What Comes First?

HONEYMOON OVER, we set out for our station in the town of Chengchiang. Yin-chang, John's serving boy, just recently married himself, had gone on ahead to get things ready for us.

We traveled down on the French Railway until about noon when we came to the spot where we were to proceed overland. Porters to carry our things and a mountain chair for me were already waiting there for us. John chose to walk. It was a beautiful trip over high velvety wrinkled mountain ranges, piled up one against another to the skyline. They afforded deep glimpses into separating valleys where quaint little hamlets lay.

It had rained for many days previously and the mountain trails were slippery. My coolies had to pick their steps so carefully that time was lost and the sun set before we were two thirds of the way. For an hour and a half we had to feel for our path with constant danger of a false step and broken bones. The last half hour the porters dared carry me no further, so down I got. Dusk was falling, so I could not see the way plainly. With John holding one arm and a Chinese coolie the other, we slid, jumped, and ran down the last slopes onto the plain.

Just as we reached the level, the moon came out and

flooded all objects in soft white light. On three sides towered dark shadowy masses—the surrounding mountains. Far off, on the fourth side, at the end of the plain, gleamed a silver sheet of water—a lake. I was so thrilled with the beauty that I sent up a thank you through the starlit sky to the Giver of every good gift.

But we still had to cross the plain. A shout ahead—and a lighted lantern approached us. It was one of the Chengchiang Christians come out in search of the missing bride and groom.

"Courage, Belle," said my dear John to very weary me. "He says that Yin-chang has a lovely Chinese feast waiting for us—been waiting for hours as I usually get in before dark when I make this trip."

So we plodded on. At length a great wall of mud and two huge massive doors loomed up before us. "Chengchiang city gate, Belle dear. They close it at 5 o'clock, but Mr. Yang told them we were coming and the watchman has orders to open for us. Not much farther now."

But I was speechless with weariness and could only stumble over the rough cobblestones of the streets until we reached a certain doorway.

"Here we are, Belle!" John called out with excitement. "Welcome home!" As he spoke, he stooped, picked me up, and carried me over the threshold and up the stairs. "This is our home! Want to see it?"

"Oh, not tonight, dear. Just give me a bed," was all I could get out, completely exhausted and faint, as we had not eaten for many hours.

"Aren't you going to come down to supper? Yin-chang has cooked such a big meal!"

But I was at the end. Words took too much strength. I just shook my head.

"Bed" was merely boards on a trestle with a mattress on top, but to stretch out and be still was pure luxury.

"Isn't there anything you can eat?" inquired my bridegroom anxiously.

I thought a moment. "Hot soup?"

"Yes, I've got a tin, I think. Just a minute," and he was gone. Shortly he was back with a big bowl of steaming hot tomato soup. Oh, was it good! It tasted like nectar—-my first meal in our own home.

The next morning I was thoroughly renewed and as keen to inspect the premises as John was to escort me around.

"I told you it wasn't much," John kept saying anxiously. And it wasn't. Two rooms over a little chapel, and right on the market street. There were no windows at all, but the front and back walls were folding doors which could be rolled back in the daytime. If you rolled them back, you got the light but no privacy. Anyone walking down the street could look right up and see in. If we wished for privacy we had to shut the doors and go into the semi-light of a closed wooden box. There was no electricity, of course.

The Asian cannot understand the Westerner's desire for privacy. Dishonest and evil deeds need to be kept out of sight, but why anything else? What do you contemplate doing that the public should not view it?

An upper back verandah, at the head of which a native stove had been built, was the kitchen. And in the side wing of the house were two small dark rooms where Yin-chang and his bride lived. The house was owned by Chinese Muslims who lived in the back wing. To do our laundry, we had to take our zinc tubs and clothes and go through the Muslims' home to the back garden where there was a well. After washing, our clothes had to be hung on our own upper and side verandahs. Anything that was not securely fastened and which happened to blow down over the railing was seized by those below as their lawful prey. I saw them using a handkerchief or towel of ours from time to time, so I was able to guess where the wind had carried our missing things!

But I was not dismayed at our poor quarters. I knew the CIM sent their missionaries to live right among the people, and I was prepared for anything. I did not mind living in a humble place for the Lord's sake. But I saw no reason why I should not make it as attractive as possible. I had come prepared with enamel paint and cretonne.

Mr. Hoste, our general director, had said something about this in my first personal interview with him. I had not understood what made him say it, but he had said: "Miss Miller, if I had a beautiful bedspread, I would throw it in the river."

I was quite startled. Did he have x-ray eyes? I did have a beautiful quilt in my boxes, a wedding gift from a girlfriend. However did Mr. Hoste know that? And if he did, why should he object? I murmured politely, "Is that so!" or some such filler-in, but inwardly I had answered, *Well, I'm not throwing my quilt into the river!* It was a lovely thing and would trim up a shack very nicely.

The windowless, wooden upstairs was an agreeable challenge. With wedding gift money we had bought some pretty rattan furniture. As a bachelor John had lived on backless benches, but now we had a small settee, a couple of chairs, a table, and a rattan rug, all in natural tones. The uneven, warped floor boards disappeared under the rug. In one corner I had to put my big trunk—there was no other place for it—but I had a pretty green and crimson traveling rug which I pinned over it as a cover. John's table/desk (off which we ate) was in another corner, and soon the dull room had blossomed into a nice living room.

When the bedroom had been fixed up in blue and

white, the place was really transformed. So began our life among the country Chinese people.

There was already a small church in Chengchiang, and John introduced me there. I was proud of his fluent Chinese and glad that one of us, at least, could speak and understand. Truly we were living right among the people. We had come for them, and they were not long in coming to us.

"Visitors, Belle!" John called out one afternoon, and a busy chatter of voices ascending the stairs brought me running. A group of peasant women who had come to market were to be my first lot of guests. I welcomed them with delight and showed them into our pretty brown and green sitting room. They admired it very much and I was glad to share it with them—or thought I was. After they were seated I began to explain the gospel message—as much as my one year and four months of language study allowed. I was thrilled to see that they understood me.

We were getting along fine when, all of a sudden, an oldish woman who was sitting on my big trunk in the corner, blew her nose with her fingers, and—wiped the stuff off on my beautiful traveling rug! In another minute a young mother laughed as she held her baby son out over my new rattan rug. She carried him to the door, but as she went she carefully held him out over the rug so that a wet streak ran down the center of my cherished floor covering. Since their own floors were of earth, my visitor had no idea she was doing anything offensive to me. That was just their custom.

Outwardly I managed to remain courteous. I escorted them to the door when they rose to leave, and in time-honored Chinese fashion begged them to go slowly and come again. Then I returned to my sitting room and stood looking at it—that disgusting gob on my traveling rug, and the discolored streak across the pretty new mat. Hot resentment rose in my heart, and there followed my first battle over things.

Suddenly I understood what Mr. Hoste had meant. "Miss Miller, if I had a beautiful bedspread, I would throw it into the river." He did not meant he did not like beautiful things. He meant that if possessions would in any way interfere with our hospitality, it would be better to consign them to the river. In other words, if your finery hinders your testimony, throw it out. In our Lord's own words, if thine hand offend thee, cut it off. He was not against our possessing hands, but against our using them to hold onto sinful or hindering things.

So I faced my choices. What was to come first in our first home? An attractive sitting room just for ourselves? Or a room suited to share with the local Chinese?

Our engagement motto hung silently on the wall—*God first*. Mentally I offered that pretty rattan furniture to the Lord to be wrecked by the country peasants if they chose. The day was not far off when we were called to leave Chengchiang and move west to Tali. Then I had an opportunity to begin anew. I sold that rug and the rattan furniture to the Chinese postmaster's wife, and our Tali guest hall was plainly furnished with the local wooden lacquer chairs and tea tables, which could be easily washed and were such as all the Chinese had.

CHAPTER FOUR
How to Develop a Taste for Bean Curd

IT HAD BEEN AGREED BETWEEN US that for the first five months after our marriage John should run the housekeeping with the help of his cook-boy, Yin-chang. There were good reasons for starting out in this topsy-turvy way:

The China Inland Mission requires that missionaries be two years on the field before uniting in marriage. This rule has been called in question from time to time, and it just had happened that we struck a period when the mission revoked the two-year rule in favor of a trial of one year. Later they returned to the two-year rule, believing it more firmly than ever. But John and I came in on this one-year trial period and decided to take advantage of it.

By this time, of course, John had been in China three years, but our superintendent, Mr. J. O. Fraser, was disappointed. "I had hoped," he said, "that you two would set an example and wait the two years anyway. Now Miss Miller will never get the language well."

If his wife's freedom to study Chinese was all that was against our marrying at the end of one year, John cheerfully offered to run the household until my third language examination was finished. He had run it in his bachelor days, so it would merely be continuing with his old routine. And with wonderful Yin-chang as cook, we anticipated no problems. As a matter of fact, I did get my language exams written off in less than the allotted period, despite Mr. Fraser's prophecy.

Our real reason for desiring an early marriage was to release me for country work and witness. Bandits abounded in the country areas in those days. Kunming had been besieged by a powerful brigand and all the single ladies had been quickly called in from the outer parts. Word was given that only married women with their husbands would be allowed to work outside the city gates. There seemed no prospect of the situation clearing soon and, as workers within the walls were many and those in the country places pitifully few, we felt we had the Lord's permission to marry and go to these needy ones. So we got married.

Good servants were scarce in Yunnan. I remember that as far back as our language school days, our principal, Mrs. Alice Macfarlane, had counseled us to begin to pray for domestic help. I had told her proudly of Yin-chang, and how fortunate I was that I would not have the servant worries such as young brides often had. She did not say much in reply, but gave me a quizzical look, for which I could not account at the moment, but remembered with understanding later.

Our days were well filled. Early every morning John held a Bible class for converts. The Lord had given us a fine group of them. An ex-actor, Mr. Yang, had been brought to Christ largely through John's witness, also a Taoist priest named Deng, and a slave girl and others. All morning I studied the language, John also having some time with the teacher. There was a street chapel in which he preached and I played the folding organ. In the afternoons we often went into the villages on the plain outside the city gate. In those days, souls were won to Christ who remained true to Him through later years of testing.

It was John who suggested our first field trip together.

Some months before our marriage, he and Tom Mulholland had heard of another valley plain about seventeen miles from Chengchiang called Yangtsung. They had paid a quick visit to it before going to Kunming for our wedding, but no one had been there since. They found a farming population with about twenty villages. As far as we know, no white man had ever been there before. The gospel message was absolutely new to them. John now proposed that we make up an evangelistic party and give a week's preaching to Yangtsung and plain. Yin-chang and his bride would go with us, and one of the recent men converts—I think it was actor Yang—to add his testimony to ours.

"This is what I've long looked forward to doing, darling," John said, "to lead you over the beautiful hills of Yunnan!" The joy of those treks for Him, with Him, and with one another, continued to highlight our married life for many years.

Arriving on Yangtsung plain we went to the market town. There was no hotel in such a small place, so they sent us to an old temple where we could sleep in an upstairs room. Yin-chang could cook for us downstairs. I was the first white woman those Chinese had ever seen, and they simply thronged us day and night. We could not eat or sleep without an audience. Boys climbed neighboring roofs to look in and watch. Exhausted after being on display from morning to night, I would go to bed, only to have women request that they might come up and talk to me while I was in bed! I would preach my one little sermon and then John or Mr. Yang would give them a good talk on the way of salvation.

During the day we went onto the plain, preaching

from village to village, but each evening we held an open-air meeting in Yangtsung market, where our temple/inn was. I had my Hawaiian guitar along and I chorded as we sang choruses and sacred songs in Chinese. One evening as I was accompanying the singing, I looked up to find our little group at the bottom of what seemed a cone of eager, living, yellow faces! The Chinese had climbed on benches, window sills, roofs, and anywhere they could, to watch the guitar. As I looked up at them, all I could see in any direction were Chinese, Chinese, Chinese—until immediately overhead my eyes at last met the tranquil beauty of the dark, star-spangled sky. Oh, what deep joy thrilled my heart! All these were listening to the old, old story, many for the very first time.

By the end of that week's effort a little group of inquirers had been called out for the Lord.

Yin-chang and his wife had nothing to do all day except cook our meals. As we ate Chinese food with them, it was no arduous task. Meal after meal there appeared only rice and bean curd. Maybe some meat, but always soybean curd. It tasted to me like squares of flannel boiled, or scorched flannel fried. At first I thought the small town produced nothing else, but as I went out early and looked I saw a lovely variety of potatoes, carrots, onions, cabbage—indeed many things for sale and quite cheap. So I asked housekeeper John to suggest to the cook a little variation from bean curd! But inevitably when we arrived at the table, there was the same old thing again. Evidently Yin-chang and his wife liked it. It was easy to prepare, no peeling like with potatoes or carrots, and they had long been accustomed to cook only what they pleased.

The last day of the week arrived and we left early in the morning to work the far end of the plain. We knew we might not be back until dark. "I'll be very hungry by supper time, John. Please make sure Yin-chang buys some potatoes and carrots! Something I can eat," I pleaded.

"All right, dear," John said, and I heard him give the order.

I set out confident that by night time I would have a square meal. It was a beautiful morning. The golden air had a cheery nip of winter in it, and the little lake at the far end sparkled its blue waters into the yellow sunshine. In the center of the plain spread the rice fields. At the rim, little hamlets were marked out by feathery green clusters of bamboo growing beside adobe houses.

From farm to farm we went. I played the guitar to draw a crowd, we all sang in Chinese, and when a group had gathered, John and Mr. Yang preached. I talked with the women and children and we gave out tracts before moving on to the next clay-walled farmyard. Everyone was friendly, but when noon came no one offered us anything to eat. I began to feel very hungry as I had not been able to eat a big breakfast when it was just rice and bean curd.

"Oh, just endure a bit, dear," John said.""This is missionary life. It takes time to walk as far as this, and I want to visit every farm at this end of the plain before we go back. Perhaps we can buy some food at the next place."

But we never could. So it continued all day long. John was four years younger than I and at the beginning of our married life he had a tendency to drive me beyond my strength, not realizing that I really did not have the physical reserves he had.

Once we were able to buy some Chinese toffee, but my empty stomach resented sweets. By the time we had returned to the inn I was faint as well as weary. I kept struggling on, thinking of meat and potatoes with perhaps some carrots.

Up the stairs of the inn we went and I was able to sit on my bed while John brought me a basin of water to wash off the dust.

"Is supper ready, Yin-chang?"

"Yes, Pastor. We will bring it right up."

It felt good to wash the dirt off. Yin-chang and wife were arranging bowls of a steaming something in the middle of the table. I came over and looked. Bean curd. Even the meat had not been cooked separately, but mixed in with the gray flannel squares!

"Where are the potatoes and carrots?" I asked.

Yin-chang looked at his wife and she looked at him. Obviously neither had paid any attention to that order. "We didn't see any on the market today," they answered, united.

"Is there nothing else to eat?" I asked, desperately disappointed.

"Nothing."

It was too much for me. I fell on my face on the bed and wept. John urged me to self-control, but I was too tired. I cried and cried, and finally cried myself to sleep.

Before midnight I woke up, my stomach gnawing with emptiness until it hurt. I sat up and hubby came over to me. "Won't you try to eat a little rice, at least, dear!" he said anxiously. "I'll get Yin-chang to heat some up for you."

"All right, I'll try a little," I said weakly. A few minutes later John handed me a bowl of warm rice with bean curd on top! But do you know, it did not taste so scorched-flannely this time. In fact, one bowl downed, I held it out for a second helping! From then on in my missionary life bean curd and I were friends. I never grew very fond of it, but it was no longer obnoxious. As it was very nutritious I often had it on our own table at home with a dish of some more tempting vegetable alongside.

This episode became a family joke. From then on, whenever some new Chinese dish appeared which did not appeal to me, my husband would be sure to say, "Maybe if you cried a little first you would enjoy it, Belle?"

The day was to come when I would learn to meet life's disappointments dry eyed. There would even be an hour when my husband himself would say wistfully that a few tears were sometimes a good thing. But it takes time to grow. And it takes more than one season to mellow.

Chapter Five
His Wonderful Cook—As Viewed by Her

Yin-chang's laziness continued to be a sore point.

I started out meaning to be a very kind mistress. Chinese never gave their servants time off; I arranged that Yin-chang and wife have a half day a week, and in every other way I watched for their comfort—until I found it was quite unnecessary! Their comfort was their own prime concern.

One piercingly cold day as I sat motionless studying with the Chinese teacher, we both became so chilled that I ordered a brazier of burning charcoal. Yin-chang was a long time bringing it and finally appeared with a tiny thing which I had never seen before. In it a few black coals were just beginning to ignite. It gave out almost no heat, so the teacher and I continued to shiver. Knowing we had a good-sized new brazier I grew suspicious, excused myself and went in search of our helpers. It was early morning and there were no servants in sight at all. So I made for their bedroom. Sure enough! There, doing nothing, sat the two of them around our big brazier piled high with red-hot coals, toasting their toes in luxurious ease. The origin of the tiny pot was obvious. They had given us theirs and spared only a coal or two to start it. No, there was no need for me to be anxiously solicitous for their welfare!

In fact, their demands increased. In that area, country Chinese never took baths in bathtubs; they did not possess such things. But these two had decided they must have everything John and Isobel Kuhn had. So I found Yin-chang one day carrying my zinc tub to their bedroom.

"What are you doing with that, Yin-chang?" I asked.

"My wife wishes to take a bath," he answered blandly.

But his wife had the itch—I was treating her for it! "Let her use the tub downstairs, then," I said. "She has the itch and it is catching. I do not wish you to use ours."

He made a sour face but had to comply.

A day or so later, after she had been into our bedroom, she came out smelling strongly of my perfume. It was the only bottle I had brought from home to help me over moments when certain odors were a little too much for me. That particular brand of perfume was not sold in our part of China! The inference was obvious, but she most indignantly denied it, saying it was her own perfume. I asked to see her bottle; as a bride she had some but it was packed away carefully in her suitcase and the scent was very different. When I pointed this out, she went to bed for two days and sulked, refusing to do any work whatever. Yin-chang declared she was ill.

Climaxes are not geysers that suddenly appear. They are mountains of small incidents, gradually piling up until they reach a peak. This time the topping experience was so trivial that I do not remember the matter at all. Yin-chang had failed in some duty, and when I pointed it out to John in the boy's presence, hoping to get it corrected, John turned on me, siding with Yin-chang.

Hot with temper, I said nothing, but put on my hat and coat and walked out of the house. Down through the town and out onto the plain I went, angry resentment boiling within. I was not going to live in a house where a lazy servant was condoned and preferred to the mistress! And so on went my thoughts. I walked for hours, blind as to direction, not caring what happened to me, just determined to get away from it all.

Finally, I was brought to myself by the curious glances of the Chinese. Little villages studded that plain and I must have been in one of them as dark was falling. It was not done! Good women were in their homes at such an hour.

For the first time, the tumult of my own feelings fell into enough quiet for that still small Voice to be heard. "You have not considered Me and My honor in all this, have you?" the Voice said. "You came to this land to make Me known. How much of Me has anyone learned from you this day, do you think?"

I was appalled. "Oh, dear Lord, I'm sorry! It is true. I've been full of myself and my hurt feelings. What can I do?"

"You can go back," the Voice said relentlessly.

I thought again of Yin-chang's smirking face and flinched. "But Lord, how can I endure the humiliation? The servants are laughing at me."

"How do you think I endure the humiliation you have brought on Me before these people?" the Voice said. "You have not invited Me into this servant situation. You've just tried to manage by your own wits."

Then and there I invited Him, humbly pleaded with Him, to work it out for me and turned my steps homeward.

What happens when the Irresistible Force collides with the Immovable Object? The first reaction was to bounce off on a path of its own. Back in the little wooden upstairs, the Immovable Object sat still at his desk. Outwardly he was studying Chinese, but inwardly a gloomy feeling that something had gone wrong with the universe depressed him. This wife of his—if she was angry, why had she not said so? In his good Pennsylvania Dutchland people spoke their minds, talked back and forth. Then a fellow could explain his side. But to flash you an angry look and then just walk out! He squirmed uncomfortably in his seat.

Where had she gone anyway? An hour or more had passed. Why didn't she come back? What if she didn't come back? The thought made him go hot all over. It would be mighty embarrassing to have to explain it to people. If there was anything he hated, it was a thing like this.

But maybe he had been a little at fault, too. If he had only waited until Yin-chang had left before he rebuked her. That was probably what had vexed her—to side with the servant in that servant's presence.

Of course, he had not actually excused Yin-chang. It had all happened so suddenly. And why did she always have to be noticing the things that were wrong with Yin-chang! He'd gotten along with him perfectly well before marriage—why not after? Of course he had never checked Yin-chang closely, and Yin-chang's wife did not seem very helpful, that was sure.

It was getting pretty dark. What if she did not—!

But at that moment she did. Conquered by the really Irresistible Force, in the door walked the so-called Irresistible Force, a humbled and grief-stricken wife.

"Oh! You're back!" What a relief! Looking at her curiously he asked, "Where did you go?"

"Out the west gate." An unusual quietness was still upon her.

"Well, it is past supper time. I've already eaten, but I'll call Yin-chang to heat yours up."

Little was said either during the meal or for the rest of the evening over Chinese study books. But each felt a gentleness in the other that had not been there before.

After their Bible reading and prayer together before retiring, the Immovable Object suddenly said, "You may dismiss Yin-chang and his wife if they bother you that much. But I do not know whom you can get in their place to help you. Servants are hard to find."

Wonder of wonders! How did such a renunciation come about? The really Irresistible Force had been at work in this heart also. What a difference when we invite Him into the situation!

"Thank you, dear. I know what it costs you to say that. I know it would mean a lot to you if we turned Yin-chang out. But really, if he is going to cause trouble between us nothing is worth that much, is it? I don't mind doing the work myself. We will just have to ask the Lord to find us another helper. Anything is better than what I've been through today." Then the bridegroom got a tender kiss in token of love's sacrifice.

It is only fair to point out that Yin-chang had not been so difficult to deal with before his marriage. When John and he were both bachelors, they did much traveling and preaching together. John encouraged him to take his turn in public witness for Christ. Thus they often stood shoulder to shoulder in open-air meetings, or sat side by side in tea shops, talking of Christ to others. This inevitably led to regard and mutual affection.

As we watched later events, it was obvious that Yin-chang got the wrong wife. She was a nominal Christian who had joined the church only to please her family. Following the Chinese custom of engaged couples rarely seeing each other, he did not know her well. Her pretty face satisfied him, and she did not reveal the proud, lazy and selfish nature behind it. Once married, all her counsel was for self-advancement. It was not hard to push Yin-chang into taking advantage of his intimacy with John. To dismiss his old comrade of the preaching trail was truly hard.

The next morning I told Yin-chang and his wife that their service was not satisfactory, and that they might go home. Of course Yin-chang went immediately to John, expecting the triumph of the day before, but did not receive it.

Yin-chang and his wife went off to their bedroom and closed the door. They did not work, but neither did they make the slightest move to leave! I could hardly wait to see the last of them, clean up the place, and get it into the order which my soul longed for. But I had yet to learn that dismissing a servant in Asia was not the simple matter it is at home.

The following morning I had my first experience of trying to light an open grate fire and cook breakfast on it. As I was struggling with the smoke and coals that would not ignite, John came up to me, took the fan, and said gravely, "I'll fan this. You are wanted downstairs."

Wondering who could want me at that early hour, and quite forgetting the regular morning Bible class, I descended the wooden stairs to the chapel beneath our two rooms. To my consternation, there was the whole church board of deacons seated looking at me, with Yin-chang, triumphant, in the background.

"Please be seated, Mrs. Kuhn," said the town postmaster, who was also the leading elder. He was very solemn and immediately began a long grave dissertation.

My heart beat with panic. It has always been easier for me to speak a foreign language than to understand it. Being nervous, I soon lost his flow of speech. "Excuse me a moment," I said. "I do not understand. May I go for Pastor Kuhn to interpret for me, please!" Turning, I flew up the stairs.

"John!" I gasped, "you've got to come and help me! Do come down and interpret for me! How can I answer when I do not understand what they've said?"

"Well," my spouse said slowly, "Guess I can do that much."

So down the two of us went, and the solemn diaconate proceeded to review this rather serious affair. The sum of the postmaster's remarks was this: they, the church deacons, had helped Pastor Kuhn secure these two Christian servants. They understood that Pastor Kuhn himself had been quite satisfied with Yin-chang's services in the past. Was that so, Pastor Kuhn?

Face grave, Pastor Kuhn bowed his head in affirmation.

But now Mrs. Kuhn says they must be dismissed. Would she kindly explain why? Had they stolen anything?

A profound silence followed. Every ear turned to hear the answer. No, they had not been dishonest.

Had there been any immoral conduct? No. What then was their crime?

Eight pairs of disapproving black eyes were fastened upon me. I felt like a culprit at the bar, and Yin-chang was grinning broadly now.

Humiliated and trembling with excitement, I tried to explain their laziness and impudence. I related the story of their using our big brazier and giving us their tiny one. But the Chinese mouths merely curled in derision. Of course servants were lazy, else they would not be in that class but would have the enterprise to set up business for themselves. What else did you expect?

Just when my hope had ebbed, and life seemed to have lost all its savor, the postmaster turned and addressed Yin-chang. "You had better pack up your belongings then, and go home."

The relief which that word brought me gave strength to see the meeting to an end. That day Yin-chang and his wife packed their things and left us.

Now I was to find out that Yin-chang had been of

some use after all. My early morning prayer time was broken into by having to light that fire on the primitive Chinese cooking stove. I had to learn from experience that when I did not balance the pots carefully and one tipped its water a little, a cloud of ashes would rise in the air and descend all over me, the stove, and the meal. If enough water happened to spill, it would put out the fire!

Breakfast finally accomplished, I must go to the market and buy meat and vegetables for the day. There were no fixed prices in those days and every single thing had to be bargained for. This gave some language practice but took far too much time. I might return home to find there had been women visitors, but after long waiting for me they had left.

John, of course, pitched in and helped me with the lighting of fires and marketing. For that first morning he felt it would be good if I learned the seriousness of dismissing servants whom the church had provided for us. And it was a lesson which I needed.

Washing up and ironing also proved time-consuming. To haul up every drop of water in a bucket from the well, try to get some heated, then sit and rub clothes by hand took hours. As often as I wiped off the flatirons, heated on the open charcoal, it seemed that a speck of soot would dance down on the shirt before me and get ironed into a black streak before I knew it had landed! I wondered how Mrs. Yin-chang had ever turned out such clean clothes for us! Often in the midst of these busy days I would hear an echo of the deacon's voice, "There are worse things than laziness."

As days went by and I felt myself unduly tied to secondary things, we began to make the servant problem a matter of prayer. The Lord needed to be invited into this affair. When He was, He took command as only He can. He sent to us a young married woman who had been deserted by her husband and left so destitute that the very clothes she had on her back were borrowed! She wasn't a Christian and her family were notoriously crooked.

But she showed me there were able Chinese servants in this world. She proved to be the cleverest, most industrious helper I ever had until I went to Lisuland. I had to show her how to do things only once, and my burden in that regard was lifted permanently. Best of all, I was able to lead her to trust the Lord Jesus as her personal Savior.

Unfortunately for me, when we were soon called to move to the west, Mrs. Chang's husband, finding her well clothed and with money in her pocket, claimed her back, and I had to leave her with him. I put her in touch with the nearest missionary and never saw her again. But I trust I shall, in heaven.

Chapter Six
Speech Seasoned with Salt

"Belle, it's come! We are appointed to move west and take over the station of Tali which has been without missionaries for a year now. Whoopee!" John waved the letter from headquarters at me with jubilation. I ran to him and we hugged each other with joyous exuberance, then stopped to join in a prayer of thanksgiving to God. The Lisu tribes of J. O. Fraser's discovery were in western Yunnan, where Tali was located.

"There's another letter," John continued. "Mr. Fraser wishes us to come up to Kunming in May. He will be there at that time and would like to see us before we go west. Also, Jack Graham and Ella are being married on May 15, and Mr. Fraser knows they want us as best man and matron of honor. So it is all working out. Then too, Bud F— is having to come to Kunming for new glasses. Belle, you will get to meet Bud at last!"

Bud had been John's special friend and confidant at Chinese Language School, 1926-28. During the term, one of their fellow-students, William Potts, had suddenly died. God had used his death to solemnize and challenge that group of new workers. Bud and John had rededicated themselves to God, and the Lord had used them to challenge others. John was especially blessed by the truth of *Christ living in the believer*. It had transformed his life.

Bud had been sent to a different province so he and I had never met. He was slim, good looking, and had dimples. Not what I would conjure up for a male saint! But as soon as you started to talk to him you forgot everything but the Lord. He lived for no one else and nothing else. In his presence my Irish effervescence soon quieted down and a great wistfulness for God came to me.

That night John was asked to preach in the street chapel, but as I was weary I went to bed instead. The evening streets brought mostly men to the chapel anyway. But before I was asleep, John burst into our room. "Belle! Say, Bud wants me to pray all night with him in the chapel. Do you mind, dear, when it is for this purpose?"

I answered slowly, "No-o, I don't mind. But I'd like to know why! Why wouldn't an hour of prayer be enough?"

"Well," said Hubby resignedly, "guess I'll have to tell you. They asked Bud and me to preach in street chapel, and as Bud went first, I couldn't help but compare his Chinese with mine. We came to China together, you know. He speaks the language okay, but I couldn't help but know that my language was better. No one responded to the gospel invitation, and the meeting finally closed. As Bud approached me, I guess I rather expected to have him compliment me on the progress I'd made since he last heard me." Here Hubby stopped and hung his head.

I was very proud of his fluent Chinese, and added, "Well?"

"Well, Bud said to me, 'John, I was disappointed tonight. You have made great progress with the language, of course, but when last I heard you speak I used to see the Christ. Tonight I could not get by John Kuhn and his fine command of the language. No one was won to Christ tonight, was there? Do you suppose you've lost something? Would you like to pray with me all night if need be—just you and me? Besides, I feel I need it. In the province where I was sent the churches are so cold. There has been argument between senior missionaries as to which Chinese term should be used for "God" in preaching and translation. Oh, is Satan going to kill our usefulness just by side-tracking us? I feel I need to pray, but I'd like to have you pray with me, as we used to do in Shanghai.' I told him that I wanted to ask you first, but I was sure you wouldn't hinder."

"I most surely won't," I replied, deeply stirred. "And tell him I'll be praying here too. It took courage to speak to you straight like that, when he was the poorer speaker of the two."

"Yes," acquiesced Hubby humbly, "but God comes first with Bud, you know. And I want that He should with us, too. I needed this correction badly."

"Bless you, dear," I said. "Go and the Lord be with you."

That all-night prayer meeting was the beginning of blessing among us all. The work in Yunnan was not dead as in Bud's province, but we'd had differences between senior missionaries, too, and our superintendent felt we all needed a fresh touch from the Lord. So he called as many together as could come, and proclaimed a cessation of all but most necessary work that the rest of the time might be spent in prayer and meeting together.

The ten days that followed we never forgot. Truly the Lord met us. The Holy Spirit convicted first one, then another. With tears we confessed critical thoughts or wrong actions to one another. There was a putting away of hindering things, with a real melting together.

This was the first time in my life that behind-the-back criticism of another Christian was shown to me to be sin—and a most deadly sin that paralyzes the Spirit, and quenches Him when He is longing to pour out blessing. I wish that I could say I was never again guilty of this, but that would not be true. It did mean, however, that from that day I recognized it as wrong and something that I must treat as sin.

Our superintendent, Mr. J. O. Fraser, was wonderful in this regard. In his speech, seasoned with salt, he was an example to all of us. He was also courageous enough to refuse to listen to criticism of another when it was made to him. Now we wonder if Bud had been afraid to say to John what he knew in his heart needed to be said, what would have been the end? We do not like to think of it.

After the conference you can imagine our anticipation as John and I started west for Tali, an old station but at the moment without missionaries. We were to continue Chinese language studies there, but also to help young missionaries whom the mission was expecting. There had been an appeal for two hundred new workers in two years, and the first of these would soon arrive. Mr. Fraser thought it was extremely important who the young missionaries spent their first years with, and we were made to feel our responsibility. John was also to itinerate and explore the areas around Tali.

Those days there was no Burma Road. We had to travel stage by stage, either walking or riding on a horse or in a *hwa-gan* (mountain chair). At night we stopped at whatever little town we had come to. It was slow, weary travel, but the beauty of the Yunnan mountains far repaid the weariness. And the opportunity to present the gospel at night in the little stopping places was worth the time consumed. I much prefer it to the dangerous ride in Burma Road trucks of later years, where you finished a week's travel in two days and lost all those little town contacts.

It was during our third stage out from Kunming that I contracted dysentery (the same kind mentioned in Acts 28:8), and was dangerously ill. We had to stop off at Tsuhsiung. An American missionary lived there in a beautiful big compound and she also had a little Christian Chinese nurse, Miss Ling, staying with her. For three weeks Miss Ling nursed me. She had nursed many such cases in Shanghai, but said she had never seen one so bad as mine. Yet the Lord brought me through.

We arrived in Tali on June 28, 1930. John had wanted me to walk with him from Hsia-kuan. Our coolies had stopped there for the night, although it was still early afternoon. The Chinese had told us that Tali was just *san-si li* (three or four Chinese miles) farther on. In fact, they meant *san-shih li*, but pronounced it differently. We thought three or four li (Chinese miles) were meant, when it actually was thirty li!

The road was level all the way and very beautiful scenery absorbed our attention. To the left rose the high range of mountains which contain the Azure Peak, 15,000 feet altitude. To the right, emerald green rice fields sloped away to a large blue lake. Tali is the marble quarry of China, and the villages through which we passed were all built of stone—quaint, picturesque dwellings. Every now and then we crossed a rushing crystal mountain stream of melted snow.

I was still weak from sickness, and it was the end of the day to boot, so I soon felt tired. But John urged me on, eager to see our new station. I went as long as I could, but when I said, "John, I can't go any farther," I meant just that.

"Oh, you're doing fine, dear, just a few more steps. See, here is the gate," he reassured me.

But I could not make those steps. He half carried me

in and laid me on the floor—the only place available, for the house was empty.

"Belle, you're awful!" he said, standing over me perplexed. "When you say you're through, you just stop. You don't make any further effort."

"But, dear," I argued weakly, "I don't say I'm through until I am!"

Help was on its way. The Chinese pastor lived in the front part of the extensive compound which was the CIM home in Tali. He soon came to see us and inquired if we had made arrangements for supper. After a long rest and some warm food, I was able to sit up, and even walk a little. John had already been all over the place. Such a domain after our two small windowless rooms in Chengchiang!

I still remember the thrill of the first evening when he led me through the rooms of the "Cloisters of Tali," as they were later named. Three wings of rooms, upper and lower, were absolutely ours. A lawn and a huge garden were at the back, not to speak of the small court between the wings, which was planted with flowering trees. It was luxury and paradise to us. Gentle, refined young Pastor Li was always so concerned for our comfort. We just loved him from the first contact on. We would preach and minister at Tali for two and a half years and there our first child would be born.

Chapter Seven
John Becomes "Daddy"

JOHN WAS ONLY TWENTY-THREE YEARS OLD when we were married, and he was not much interested in babies. He wanted to be able to take me around with him when he itinerated.

But at the end of our first year, I knew God was going to give us a child. I broke the news with a bit of inner perturbation. Would John be vexed? I would have many surprises yet to come from this same "Daddy." He was delighted.

A radiant light beamed on his face. "Great news!" he cried out. "I hope it's a boy. Then when the Chinese ask me, 'Pastor Kuhn, have you any children?'"—and here he repeated the typical Chinese phrase—"I'll be able to answer, '*Yu ih-ko; yu ih-ko hsiao tu-shu-ti*' (Yes, one—a small schoolboy)."

I did not want John to get his heart set on a boy. What if it turned out to be a girl? "Yes, but what if you have to answer: 'It's a small cook-rise-to-eat one' (*Hsiao chu-fan-ch'ih-tih*)?"

"Oh, that will be all right too," answered the thrilled and happy Daddy-in-prospect. "But where is the baby to be born? The nearest hospital is Kunming. Are you going all that long way back? It will be only a year since we left there! I don't like to go trotting back to the capital city so soon. It would take a big scoop out of our time."

"That's what I think, too," I replied. "I've been thinking of Miss Ling, at Tsuhsiung. She nursed me through dysentery, remember? I happen to know that she is a midwife with lots of experience, trained by Dr. Mary Stone of Bethel Mission in Shanghai. She'd be capable, I'm sure!"

"The very one!"

So it was arranged. John, who had now become skilled in Chinese writing, carried on the correspondence with Miss Ling.

John and I had no idea we were doing anything hazardous. That a woman expecting her first baby needs more medical check-ups than others had never occurred to us. Mails were overland and slow; there was no airmail to those parts. So it was a long, long time before we learned how anxious some of the older women in the mission were that I had not seen a doctor, did not plan to see one, and was trusting everything to a Chinese nurse! By that time, it was too late to get me out to a hospital, so they did what remained to do. They prayed hard for us! And I came through wonderfully.

It was March, 1931 when Miss Ling arrived. Already we had junior workers. Ernest Mansfield and Will Allen had been studying Chinese under John's tutoring for some months by that time. They were two young bachelors, full of devotion to the Lord, but also blessed with a sense of humor, which helped us fit in to one another. Ernest was Australian, Will English, but born in China and educated at our CIM school at Chefoo.

Miss Ling was a slight, small young woman with a business-like manner. She had a book on obstetrics with her and showed me the gruesome pictures in it of unnatural presentations and instrument cases. I wished she had not—they haunted me! Now I knew what was possible, and I shuddered. But she was very casual.

"Oh, don't worry. I've delivered each of these special cases, and all by myself too! It is experience that counts. Now you will probably have long labor at your age (29). Walk! Get out and exercise those muscles. Limber them up!"

Sensitive to grinning Chinese with knowing looks, I hunted for a place to walk. There I went every morning, walking back and forth, praying or studying Chinese for several hours at a time. Much did I pray for the little "boy-student" or "girl-cook" who was coming to us. I had been reading a book in which the author said, "But Elspeth was God's child alway" (*Sentimental Tommy* by James Barrie). I liked that. So I asked it for our firstborn. "May he or she be God's child always!"

When the time came, Miss Ling had everything prepared in our own big, airy bedroom on the second floor. She was very efficient, but as the first pains made me catch my breath and wince, she said, "Oh, that's nothing! They'll get much worse than that!"

It was my dear husband who was my pillar of strength at that trying hour. I will always bless him for his faithfulness, tenderness and strength when I had to go down into the valley for our babies. He stayed with me all the time, holding my hand on one side while Mrs. Li, our Chinese Bible woman held the other. John's grip was like the rock of Gibraltar, but Mrs. Li's grasp, swaying on her tiny bound feet as she did, was like hanging onto a paper scarf! She prayed incessantly for me in Chinese: "Oh God, help!" But it was the silent solidity of my husband's grip that seemed to pull me through.

At 11:40 P.M., April 10, 1931, a thin wail pierced the lamp-lit room and Kathryn Ann Kuhn had made her appearance in this old world.

As soon as baby was taken away by nurse to be bathed, John knelt and, taking my hand, thanked our dear Lord for the merciful delivery, and for our little daughter. "And Lord," he prayed, "we give her back to You. We lay no claim to her. We want her to be Yours and to serve You all her life."

It was not long before Nurse Ling returned with a small red-faced bundle. Babies are notoriously ugly their first twenty-four hours; they usually resemble small boiled lobsters, or little wrinkled old men. Kathy was no exception. As I looked at the little wrinkled face, I wondered, *Will John like her? He is such a lover of beauty.*

I was to spend hours chuckling at his surprising reaction. John got down on his knees to get closer and cried eagerly, "What do you think, Belle? Who is she like?"

Out of compassion for him, I was going to suggest that she looked like me when Nurse Ling interrupted. "She looks like *muh-si*. Don't you see she has those scooped-out (deep-set) eyes?"

You should have seen the radiant smile that swept over his face! He fairly beamed at Miss Ling. "Did you hear, Belle? Miss Ling says she looks like me! I think she does, too. You know," he continued confidently, "They say that the child always takes after the stronger character of the two!"

I was awakened the next morning by a call from baby's alcove. It was John's voice. The window in the alcove opened close to Ernest Mansfield's. John had been waiting to see if Ernest was awake. As soon as he discerned movement, he called out, "Ernest!"

From my bed I could see Ernest's face come to the window. Then John held up his arms with something cradled in them. "It's born!" he said in ecstasy. "It's a girl! I'll bring her over for you to see."

"Oh, don't bother, she might catch cold," Ernest called back. "I'll come over to your place. I'll call Will, too."

I smiled at my husband's boyishness. No new toy

had ever caught his boyhood fancy and swung him off his feet like that little girlie. I could see her face was still red and wrinkled and wondered how the two bachelors were going to salve their consciences and yet please their senior missionary.

Ernest, always kind and sympathetic, had done some successful thinking on his way up the stairs. "Oh, isn't she a dear!" he exclaimed enthusiastically.

Daddy beamed. Enthusiasm was all he needed; the reasons for it were not important. Then John turned expectantly to Will. "They say she looks like me," he suggested hopefully.

Will's transparent honesty was knocked off balance. He gave a quick laugh. "Oh come now, John, you really—"

But sympathetic Ernest had been bending over baby. He straightened and said, "Yes, I think she does, John. The shape of her head is yours, round with a square jaw. Isobel's head is long and thin, and the jaw almost pointed. Yes, that jaw declares her a Kuhn!"

"You really think so, do you?" murmured Daddy complacently. He was sublimely happy, and the bachelors' visit had been a great success.

Kathy's redness faded soon, of course, and the wrinkles smoothed out. The little cheeks became apple-blossom velvet. From the first she had beautiful black curly eyelashes. When the time came that she began to laugh, her hazel eyes sparkled like topaz. Charm is a thing difficult to describe, but Mommy somehow thought she was going to have that when she grew up.

It is not Asian custom to show a baby to visitors during the first month. In fact, among the Chinese peasants of those parts, and among the Lisu too, even the mother was not available to friends for the first four weeks. But Daddy burst all such bounds. Our wonderful baby was the first topic of conversation and, sleeping or not, must be produced for every visitor.

One morning while we were discussing a Chinese name for our baby, someone was playing the gramophone. The song was "Grace that is greater than all our sins." As the chorus floated up to us, "Grace, grace, God's grace..." both of us, almost simultaneously, exclaimed, "There it is! Let's call her Hong-En (Vast-Grace) in memory of God's goodness to us."

She was dedicated to God in the chapel at Tali at the end of thirty days. It happened that the country pastor, Mr. Li, had a baby girl named Heo-En (Great-Grace), also one month old. So the Chinese and American babies were dedicated at the same time, we parents also standing up together. Of course, we gave a feast to the Chinese to celebrate our little girl's one-month birthday.

TWELVE YEARS PASSED before Daddy had a repetition of the joy of fatherhood. We had hoped to have a second child who would be a playmate for Kathy. But due to over exertion during a time of stormy flood and fright, I lost that hope.

It was with a very different scare that Danny appeared. We were then in the wild canyon of the Upper Salween, and the Japanese War was in full spate. In fact, the Japanese were just across the river from us. To go out to the hospital would mean not returning until the war was over. One had to get a military pass from the Chinese Government to come into the mountain area where we lived. They would never give such permission to a woman and her baby. If I went out I must stay out. But I had just been definitely led into the canyon.

Then God worked. Miss Dorothy Burrows, one of our English nurses at Tali hospital, was due a vacation. She loved the tribes work and volunteered to come, taking that in lieu of her vacation. A Chinese guerrilla colonel had offered to get her a military pass and escort her in! Truly it seemed of the Lord.

Once again, I did not once see a doctor, but was very efficiently cared for by an experienced nurse. But this confinement was not ordinary. I was nearly forty-two years old and conditions arose which took expert skill. The baby chose to appear on Sunday, August 1, 1943, just as the Lisu were leaving church. We were living at Maliping (Oak Flat Village) and many from surrounding villages came there for the noonday service.

We had been hoping for a son, so Nurse Burrows was jubilant as she brought the little bundle to me, saying, "It is Daniel, all right!"

"Now I can answer the Chinese, 'One of each' when they ask if I have children!" Daddy exclaimed.

That was the first inkling I had that he felt the stigma of not having a son. For twelve years he had been politely asked about his children and had been forced to answer, "Only one, a daughter."

To see big Daddy walking around with the little golden head resting in the crook of his arm was a thrill I never forgot. He wanted to take his son everywhere: to watch the volleyball game at play hour, to go for a walk over the mountainside. And when they came back there was a wild flower set into the tiny fist "for Mommy."

His name had been chosen for love of the young Jewish prophet who "purposed in his heart not to defile himself." For the Chinese and Lisu to pronounce "Daniel" was simple. Their Bibles transliterate it Da-nay-lee.

Chapter Eight
Counting Raindrops

IT WAS IN TALI that I learned to count raindrops. The first anniversary of our wedding had seen us welcome our first junior workers, Ernest Mansfield and William Allen. From then on we were alone almost never again.

It was great preparation for them. John and I occupied the large room in the central wing, but the eastern wing of the house looked out on wonderful old mountain peaks. They spoke of the steadfastness as well as of the power of our God. There were three little upper bedrooms, so Ernest and Will each had one, with the middle room making a nice sitting room for them.

These were busy days and we all came together at meals, eager for a little social break from language study and new converts classes.

It was during one of these meal times that my husband chose to correct me publicly. I was in the beginning of some adventure we had shared together and was sketching the background before my real story began. "And it was pouring rain" went my background, when John stopped me.

"I don't remember that it was pouring with rain," he announced firmly. "I'm afraid you exaggerate at times, Belle. As I remember the occasion, it was merely raining."

"Well," I replied, indignant at having my perfectly

good story spotlighted on mere minor detail. "I didn't stop to count the raindrops, I—"

"But that is just what you should do," said my incorrigible husband. Turning to Will and Ernest, he continued. "I'm afraid Isobel exaggerates sometimes and I want to help her get out of this habit."

Now I was careful as to truth, but as artists do when painting a picture, I highlighted it sometimes to give the correct impression. I did not even know I had the habit, but it had bothered John for some time.

Will and Ernest enjoyed seeing John bait his wife and aided him with delight. Three to one, I did not stand a chance. That was the beginning of a very drastic, grueling course in the art of factual storytelling. At first it was only John who would suddenly stop me as I began to relate an experience with that soon-hated question, "Did you count the raindrops?" After a while, the others took it up. If I told a dinnertime story that happened to cap someone else's, Will or Ernest would grin and say, "Isobel didn't stop to count the raindrops that time." It never failed to produce laughter—and a united male front!

Finally, I became so sensitive and hurt about what I thought was an attack on my truthfulness that I decided to stop taking part in mealtime conversations altogether. Maybe they did not notice it, but I dropped out of the storytelling rounds. I was hurt and I felt they had been unnecessarily cruel.

But as I have looked back on it from the softening influence of the years, I have thanked God for this experience.

I had been a literature major at varsity. In fiction, it is true that to obtain the effect of a real situation, one has to highlight certain aspects. But God was preparing to use my pen to relate stories of His work in human hearts. He could not afford to let my pen grow careless with the facts. I needed a stern lesson to make me afraid of inaccuracy—and I got it! It was very unpalatable, but it was very much needed.

My husband was young and zealous to "rule well his own house" (I Timothy 3:4). He has always censored my writings, checking for accuracy in detail, especially in our circular letters. In those early years, circular letter writing day was a grueling time for me. Every word I wrote was challenged. One result was that our circular letters of those days did not bless people; they were rarely quoted in the mission magazine and the work did not come alive for the prayer helpers.

Imagination must not play with facts, we all agree to that, but it has its place in interpreting heart attitudes of people. If imagination recreates the scene, keeping true to the general gist of the conversation, immediately the characters leap into life. But my critic would raise the red pencil and say, "Is this word for word what each person said?" *Count your raindrops!*

"My dear husband," the poor writer would say with a sigh, "I do not know shorthand. I did not take it down verbatim. None of us knew that the conversation was going to be a turning point. But you yourself know that this was, in general, how the conversation went."

"All right," my husband would respond, "You say so. Say that this is your interpretation of the conversation."

"But that is perfectly ridiculous," I would wail. "Every reader knows that a conversation cannot be remembered word for word. What I have written was the decision made at that meeting, now wasn't it? And if the questions and answers are faithfully in character, it does not need to be verbatim. If I stop my story to explain, it will spotlight interest on *me*, distract the reader, and interfere with the flow of sympathy toward the main character."

But down would come the red pencil and imagination was slain. So we continued for several years.

I want you to note this, because similar situations are not uncommon among all young couples. If we will just be patient with one another, God will work for us.

Gradually, the knowledge that everyone does not see the same scene with the same eyes grew on my husband. Just because I had noticed a beautiful sunset on an occasion when he hadn't—perhaps because he was preoccupied in a discussion with someone—didn't mean there had been no sunset!

Also, the Lord began to show him that his wife had a gift for making a situation live to others. Frequently at the dinner table he would call on me to relate a family anecdote, because people saw the point more vividly when I described it. In other words, he began to sense a difference in our gifts. He was learning to give me the freedom of personality. Eventually the red pencil became more cautious in what it struck out, and friends at home began to write of the blessing they had received from the circulars. Some even asked that the circulars be printed!

On the other hand, I had become more careful about accuracy in what I termed the unimportant matters. To me the important thing was the general truth of the story. If I could sketch the main figures vividly and truthfully, I was content. I did not always remember accurately the little details of the background. Before my marriage, this had been of no importance to me. But the Immovable Object had shown me that a Christian writer cannot be too particular that every point be according to reality.

The result has been a mutual recognition of each other's gifts. Now I am always anxious that John check what I have written, for I still make mistakes in the "unimportant" things.

Until the Lord is able to work out in us a perfect adjustment to one another, we must bear with one another, *in love*.

I feel many modern marriages are wrecked on just such a sharp shoal. A human weakness is discerned. It is pointed out, but the correction is resented or airily dismissed as unimportant. That grates. The second time of default, the rebuke is sharper. Perhaps it contains a sting. This is resented and the argument grows bitter.

With novels and movies which teach false ideals of marriage, young people are not prepared "to bear and forbear." They are not taught to forgive. The are not taught to endure. Divorce is too quickly seized upon as the only way out.

It is the worst way out! To pray to God to awaken the other person to where he or she is hurting us, to endure patiently until God does it: *this* is God's way out. And it molds the two opposite natures into one invincible whole. The passion for accuracy plus a sympathetic imagination which relives another's joys and sorrows—that is double effectiveness. Either quality working unrestrained by itself would never had been so effective. But it cost mutual forgiveness and endurance to weld those two opposites into one! Let's be willing for the cost.

Chapter Nine
Unwanted Assignment

In 1931, some months before Kathryn was born, our nearest missionaries, ten days' journey west at Paoshan, gave us an invitation to come over and help them in a special evangelistic effort at their station. The call "Westward Ho!" has always stirred our blood, so we accepted joyfully.

On such trips John usually rode a horse or walked and I rode a mountain chair. One particular afternoon we were winding up and over mountaintops for a long time. I was wondering where we would sleep that night. The sun had begun to lower, yet we were still wandering over wild uninhabited mountains. Suddenly, John, who was walking a little distance ahead of me, disappeared. I got out of the mountain chair and began to walk, hoping to speed up my slow carriers. I hallooed John, but there was no answer. He had turned to wave to me just before going around the crest of a peak, so I hurried up that little slope, turned the corner and—gasped.

The mountain fell away from my feet in a steep drop to tiers of lower hills of graduating heights, like colossal steps descending. There, far below, was John, a mere speck on the path that circled one of the tiers before it dropped to the next hill. He turned to look for me, saw me, and waved.

The range had given way to a beautiful little green valley, at least two thousand feet beneath us. Through the valley ran a stream, shining like a silver ribbon through emerald fields with sunset glory gilding the opposite mountain bank. From the other side of the valley rose tier after tier of hills until it leveled off even with where I now stood. It made me feel as if I was on top of the world.

It was the valley of Yungping, meaning Eternal Peace. We were to spend the night in the little market town that huddled against the foot of the western hills. Far below me John was signaling with his arms that I should hurry up. Reluctant to leave that most wonderful panorama, I knew by the setting sun that I must. So down the grassy slopes I ran.

The population was mostly Muslim. That night, after our supper, we went out on the street for an open-air meeting, as was our custom. But the audience was unmoved, stony-faced and indifferent. John felt depressed.

As we prepared for bed in the dusty little inn, he said to me, "I suppose someone will be asked to come here and open this plain to the gospel. A missionary has never lived here, so there has never been a thorough presentation of the message. I pity the person that has to tackle this job. Maybe Mr. Fraser will ask Will to come here." Will Allen was noted among us as always rising to the occasion.

Neither John nor I dreamed that we would be the ones Mr. Fraser would assign to this difficult task. Yet it was so.

Mr. Fraser had never intended that missionaries should stay on in an old established work like Tali. The Chinese Christians should run their own church eventually, and there were still many large areas of West Yunnan unevangelized. Therefore, when the last batch of "Forward Movement" workers had been sent to us, Mr. Fraser suggested that we ourselves open up a new district. Eternal Peace was the place he named.

I have seldom seen my husband more downcast. He had loved the work at Tali. For him it had been a joy to explore the needy fields around Tali, to help in the initial preaching efforts. Now to be confined to one valley of such indifferent and difficult people as Muslims!

To me the appointment was quite agreeable. I had fallen in love with the beautiful little plain. I was also glad to get back to life nearer the nationals. Tali was on the main road of travel, and for me as hostess there was much entertaining of missionaries of other missions, not to mention world explorers and hunters. I had lost several of my Chinese Bible classes through the constant interruption of unexpected Western visitors.

I was also happy at the prospect of an area big enough for a life work, but small enough that I would always get back home by nightfall and sleep in my own clean bed! I did not like travel. But I felt sorry for John.

The work in the church and country around Tali had been thriving, but now blessing seemed to leave and sickness struck us. We had recently received four young men as new workers when I came down with a fever we could not diagnose. There was no doctor nearer than Kunming, at that time a two-week journey away. Nurse Ruth Colquhoun (later Mansfield) was summoned from Mitu.

She came gladly, but she had never seen a fever like it. Searching the medical books she felt that blackwater fever was the nearest in description to what I was experiencing.

I grew steadily weaker and John became concerned for my life. As he knelt at my bed praying that I might be allowed to recover, the Lord spoke to him about his own inner unwillingness for our new assignment.

There was a keen struggle. Then he yielded.

I began to improve. But I was exceedingly weak when the fever left me and almost had to learn to walk anew.

St. Francis de Sales said, "If He calls you to a kind of service which is according to His will but not according to your taste, you must not go to it with less, rather with more courage and energy, than if your taste coincided with His will."

Blessing began to flow again. There is a definite relationship between inner surrender and outward blessing, which is another proof of a living God, who can read the innermost heart. Outwardly John had accepted the assignment graciously and fellow workers were witnessing as zealously as ever, yet a sudden tightness had come, which only began to loosen again after his private surrender.

In those two and a half years at Tali (1930-32) we received ten new workers, helped them get through their first language exams, rented premises, and assisted them to get started in six different towns, including Yungping. Each place had a whole plain full of Chinese until then unevangelized. Besides, in and around Tali souls were saved, John and I finished the required language examinations, and Kathryn was born to us.

Chapter Ten
Beginnings at Yungping

AT THE NORTHERN END of the plain of Yungping was a little town called Old Market. The population here was not so wholly Muslim, and John was blessed in obtaining an old native house on the river bank. It had three wings around a little courtyard. The fourth side was the river walk. The unwashed dirt of years lay everywhere and the walls were black with soot.

John was disheartened at the task of cleaning it up and repairing it, but I saw possibilities in its spaciousness, and loved the privacy of the river bank. "Don't worry," I assured him gaily, "Sally and I will soon clean it up and transform it!"

Sally Kelly, who later became Mrs. Stuart Harverson, was our newest young worker. She was to live with us during her first language study days. She was a Scottish girl from my own home town of Vancouver. Unselfish, capable and devoted, she also sparkled with wit and humor. The longer we knew her the more we loved her.

God prospered us, too, in getting the help of two fine Chinese carpenters, a father and son. They not only repaired the house, putting in wooden floors and windows, but also made furniture for us. They charged a lump sum for two months' labor, and as they were very industrious, it made the cost of repairs and furniture quite reasonable.

There had also been the matter of servants. John was for waiting until we got to Yungping where we could hire some local residents and train them. But Kathryn was about a year-and-a-half old when we moved to Yungping—just the toddling age when she must be watched carefully, especially as we lived so near the river.

I had been warned by someone born a child of CIM missionaries never to leave my children to national amahs, or let unbelievers play with them promiscuously. Evil habits and speech can be learned in early childhood and are difficult to eradicate later. So I was always very careful and watchful with my little one.

Our cook, Mrs. Hwang, was a widow with only one child, a daughter about thirteen years old. The daughter, Small Pearl, was a spoiled child, but she was a pure little thing and took care of our small Kathryn. So I wished to bring mother and daughter with us to Yungping.

"You know that Mrs. Hwang is not satisfactory," John argued.

"Yes," I replied, "but who is to market and cook and watch Kathryn while we clean that sooty house? I will be in no situation to train raw hands during the first week or so."

"All right, have it your own way," my hubby said good-naturedly. "But I'm afraid you'll be sorry." And oh, wasn't I!

Mrs. Hwang worked well at first, and certainly did relieve me during the cleaning period. And Small Pearl was always reliable in caring for little Kathryn.

Downstairs in the central wing was to be the Chinese guest hall and dining room, with a small room at the side for John's study. The long black hole upstairs was to be our bedroom. The carpenter put in a window or so, and then we set out to clean the room.

It had been the ancestral worship hall, and placed against the wall was a long buffet-like table where idols had stood. There was no ceiling. Long soot-encrusted cobwebs hung from the roof tiles.

With hair tied up in a kerchief and broom in hand, Sally mounted the table to sweep the roof. She struck a dramatic attitude, and with outflung arm began, "Behold I—!"

Crash! The house shook. Black soot rained down upon us, and I thought for a second that the end of the earth had come. I had instinctively shut my eyes in self-defense, but when I opened them, I saw in horror a heap of soot-blackened rags on the floor before me. Out from the top of them stared two startled sky-blue eyes. They were the only part of Sally Kelly still recognizable. The rest looked like the dirtiest chimney sweep Scotland had ever produced.

The table had a broken leg and Sally's hundred pounds had caused it to collapse. But the weight of the fall so shook the house that it acted as a roof cleaner. The soot of many years was knocked off and descended upon us.

When we realized no bones had been broken and saw that our roof was so unexpectedly cleaned for us, we laughed till we shook again. This was typical of those days of repairing the breaches in Eternal Peace.

Soap, water and whitewash effected quite a transformation. Of course, visitors were not lacking, and one of us was always free to witness to them.

We expected it would prove a hard place, so you can imagine our feelings when one afternoon a great racket outside our gate startled us and brought us all running. Through our front gate a procession marched.

First came boys setting off firecrackers. "Pop! pop! bang! bang!"

"What's going on?" John muttered, going forward to receive them.

Behind the fireworks was a single file of the leading citizens of Old Market, each carrying a tray with gifts on it! There was a handsome pair of scarlet satin scrolls on one, packages of sugar or tea on others, and so on.

Mystified but gracious, John showed them into the guest room and relieved them of the trays. The leading townsmen had come to welcome us to Eternal Peace, and they all meant to join us! They had heard about the Christian church and they noticed that Pastor Kuhn did not drink or smoke. Fine morality! They were all for it too, but gradually, of course. Buddhism was old-fashioned, they realized, and it would be wise to have something more modern, just like a benefit society, you know. They all beamed at John.

It was difficult, but also an excellent opportunity. John explained that Christianity was not a new kind of club, but a personal relationship with God, based on His forgiveness of our sins. All men are sinners.

"Yes, yes," they nodded in grave assent, thinking this was Pastor Kuhn's way of referring to wine and tobacco.

But when he got to, "Thou shalt have no other gods before me," they began to talk. Perhaps idols were old-fashioned—they could go. But, of course Pastor Kuhn would not ask them to give up ancestor worship. Why, that was the basis of Chinese culture! Confucius and Christ could get along quite well together, could they not?

They were politely incredulous when told that Christians may worship no one but God—most decidedly not ancestors, who were but creatures of His creation. "We may venerate our ancestors but not worship them," John said.

In embarrassment they took their leave.

After John had politely escorted them to the door and warmly urged them to come again for more discussion, he returned to us. "Did you ever see a more vivid illustration of what I've been reading these days? Campbell Morgan was saying in *The Acts of the Apostles*, 'Satan's first choice is to cooperate with us. Persecution is only his second-best method.'"

From then on the work at Eternal Peace was just as difficult as we had preconceived it. Several illiterate peasant women were won to the Lord, and a young fellow named Ma Fu-yin, who could read.

His death before he was thirty left the little group of Christians without a leader. It was not until Communism took over years later, and with all the white missionaries gone, that an educated Chinese lady was led of the Lord to go to Eternal Peace. There she gleaned a harvest from seed long sown and watered with prayers, and we heard that a little church was thriving in Eternal Peace, led by this Christian Chinese lady. But this is moving ahead of our story.

At first, our cook was quite helpful. But as new young workers came to live with us, Mrs. Hwang relapsed into her old laziness. She would not buy or prepare enough food. She would not make bread when told to, but ran it so short that frequently we had to go a meal or so without any because her new batch had not risen. And so on. It caused me almost as much trouble as if I had to do it all myself. More and more she became a thorn in the flesh.

But when I spoke of dismissing her, she immediately made preposterous claims. I must pay her for travel by sedan chair back to Tali and pay for an escort, as she was afraid to go alone. Then I would have to pay for a sedan chair for Small Pearl, too, and coolies to carry their things. I had brought her so far from home, I was responsible for getting her back. She made conditions that were impossible for us to fulfill, so we had to keep her on. Yet she grew worse and worse, and quarreled with everyone. I had to redo her work daily until I was groaning with the bondage of it.

Then I began to commit the situation to the Lord. "Father, I confess I was wrong not to take John's advice at the beginning. He said I would rue it, and I do. But is there no help for me now? I can't get rid of her, but You could. Please take her from me."

He did not choose to answer immediately. I was praying daily to be relieved of her for some three months before the freedom actually came.

Meanwhile, Mrs. Hwang began to quarrel with everyone around her. She grew more and more cantankerous until the neighbors became angry with her and the women in the market turned against her. Of course she never admitted she was wrong. It was always everybody else who was mean! But with everyone everywhere disliking her, she became so unhappy that she quit one day of her own accord! She had met some horsemen from Tali who were going back, and she hired a horse for herself.

To me, it was like a miracle.

Little Pearl was in tears. She had found her mother difficult to live with too, and she wanted to stay with us. We offered to keep her as Kathryn's nursemaid, and her mother, uncertain of her own future and expenses, gave consent. So the morning came when the mother departed.

The whole household decided to celebrate and have a spring cleaning. Mrs. Hwang had been supposed to do the sweeping and dusting, but as with everything else, it had been done very negligently. Now we all set to and cleaned the house thoroughly. John insisted we have our pictures taken—heads tied up in bandannas, brooms, dustpans and scrubbing pails well to the fore.

Oh the fun of those days when we were all young!

The years proved Small Pearl to be the jewel of our work at Yungping. She confessed the Lord and asked for baptism. Up to that time, we had baptized none at Yungping. We did not baptize on a mere profession of faith, but only after testing for sincerity and carefully instructing the applicant in its meaning.

For the rite of baptism, John chose a site at the river. As this would be in full view of the busy market, however, he decided that Small Pearl should be baptized very early in the morning, before people were abroad.

There happened, however, to be an early bird. A Chinese woman opposite us opened the door that morning to behold a procession issuing from the white man's house across the river. First came Pastor Kuhn, recognizable by his height and build. Then came Small Pearl. After her Mrs. Kuhn, Miss Kelly, Mrs. Yang, and a string of Chinese—the Christians probably. Pastor Kuhn and Small Pearl entered the river, the others stood on the bank. Then the Pastor took the child and swung her beneath the water!

The astonished spectator only watched long enough to assure herself that Small Pearl was allowed to get out alive, when she waddled off to awaken her neighbor to this alarming bit of gossip. In a few hours the whole market buzzed with it.

Some of the more courageous ones came over to our house to ask, "What has Small Pearl been doing that she should be treated to such a harsh punishment?" The Christian ritual of baptism was then explained. Alas, not everyone chose to be convinced! But some believed.

Small Pearl later became the Mrs. Yang, the schoolmasters' wife, in the story, *Nests Above the Abyss*. She was a godly woman, knowing victory in affliction, and was a real soul winner. Our two years in Yungping were worthwhile if they had given us only Small Pearl.

Chapter Eleven
The Forgotten Cloak

WE HAD BEEN AT YUNGPING about a year when a letter came from our superintendent asking John to escort a sick missionary out to Kunming. As I had been suffering from back and headaches it was decided that I go too and consult a doctor.

Traveling overland by mountain chair, we usually stopped at whatever mountain village we came to at dusk. As the villages were very primitive in style, accommodation was indifferent. Dark dusty inns made you glad to get out on the road again the next morning. Our noon meal was purchased at whatever place had any food for sale about midday—rice, vegetables, or perhaps even meat, served on uncovered wooden tables, with chickens and dogs dashing around our feet for scraps which might fall from our rice bowls.

I was always glad to get baby Kathryn, due to have her second birthday when we reached Kunming, out of such places and into her mountain chair again. Possibly that was the reason I forgot to pick up my raincoat at one such noon stop and calmly walked off without it!

That afternoon we descended a steep hill, on the top of which sat the village where we had our noon meal. Down, down we went. Mountaintops and ridges surrounded us. I thrilled with the beauty of the scenery. The road dipped into a little valley through which a stream wandered. Then we climbed again, but not so high. We skirted the side of the hill for some minutes, then turning a corner came upon Hwang Lien Pu.

It was a village comprised of mud or wooden houses on each side of the main road for perhaps half a mile—that was all. Where to find the sleeping place that was least dirty, least smoky, was always our problem, and having found it, to get our beds in order before nightfall.

It was when we were unpacking and arranging our things that I realized I had left my raincoat at the noon stopping place. "Oh, John!" I cried, rushing out impetuously to lay hold of my tired husband. "I've forgotten my raincoat! It was drizzly this morning, you know, and I had it with me when we stopped for lunch. It is still quite early in the afternoon; do you think you could...?"

"No, I can't!" John said, not waiting for me to finish. He was tired out and still had some dickering with the coolies to go through. They probably wanted "meat money"—a generous tip.

I had not intended to ask *him* to go back up that long hill for my coat. We had the young Chinese boy, Ma Fu-yin with us, and I had thought to offer him some extra money to go after my garment. He was only about twenty years old and that climb would be nothing to his strong young limbs bred to these hills. That particular raincoat was more expensive than I had usually purchased, but my father had urged me to get it, since it must last seven years.

"But I can't lose it, John," I argued, probably with heat. "That coat cost money. Someone has got to go back for it. Couldn't Ma Fuh-yin?"

But John himself needed the lad as middleman to placate the chair coolies. "No, I'm not going to send Ma," he answered shortly. He looked The Immovable

Object. When he got that expression on his face I knew further talk was useless.

"All right, I'll go myself. Take care of baby," I said and flounced out of the inn and down over the path by which we had first come. I was angry, but soothed my conscience by telling myself again the price that had been paid for that coat.

The sun was still warm on my shoulders as I wound my way around the mountain and down to the stream. The steep climb was plainly in view on the opposite hill. I knew the village was at the top, though out of sight. But I had forgotten how long it took to get even to the foot of the climb.

By now the sun had gone down and in Yunnan there is no long twilight. Night comes swiftly on. I began to toil up the steep grade, panting and gasping. Coming down had been easy. I did not realize it would be so difficult to climb! Dusk turned into dark, and still I struggled up that ascent.

Tired out, I had to sit down to get my breath. Something rustled in the forest above me and I went cold with dread. I looked up the road I still had to go and saw that I was merely at the foot of it. By far the greater part of the climb was yet to come. Back at the inn at Hwang Lien Pu they would have eaten supper by now, and I was faint for want of food. I had rushed off without taking any money. I had no bedding and even if I managed to reach the village at the top of the hill I could not pay for lodging or food. I was crazy to go on. I must just eat humble pie and go back.

"Two years ago," said a Voice in my heart, "you bounced off just like this, to your sorrow. You promised me then you wouldn't do it again."

"Yes, Lord, but he would have let my expensive raincoat be lost!" I defended myself, still sure I was right. The Voice of the Lord was stifled.

All this time my feet were wearily retracing the path to Hwang Lien Pu. It was so dark by now that I was a bit nervous at being alone on the wild mountains. As I climbed up onto the Hwang Lien Pu trail I saw a light ahead, swinging back and forth. Two men came towards me carrying a lantern. You can imagine my relief and joy when I found it was John and Ma Fuh-yin.

"Well, dear, we were coming out to search for you," said Hubby in a kind voice.

"Thank you, I appreciate that. But I didn't make it. I got too tired."

"Don't worry, dear. Ma Fuh-yin has promised to go early tomorrow morning. I'll pay him extra for it. I'm sure he will be able to get the coat. You must be very hungry."

It was only love and kindness that met me. But I had learned a lesson: the Lord was able to move John where I could not. In future differences of opinion I was to count on that. Besides, I learned that it is foolish to get excited over a negative answer from a man who is tired, hungry and harassed. If I had just waited until John's own problems were settled, of course he would have been reasonable!

I also learned to beware of precipitate action, to which my Irish disposition is so prone and which is such a trial to my deliberate husband. Quick, impulsive action almost always ends in humiliation and failure.

Chapter Twelve
A Hard Day

A YEAR HAD PASSED. Suddenly the way opened for us to leave Chinese work to junior colleagues, two young ladies who returned with us from that trip to Kunming. We were free to enter the Lisu work.

As it would be very rough living, Mr. Fraser thought I ought to make a trial trip in to see the conditions before planning to move in permanently. Also, there was pressure on the new believers to plant opium in the Oak Flat area, where Leila Cook worked alone. (Allyn Cooke was six days north of her in the canyon, teaching and consolidating a new work there.) A white man's presence might remind the local feudal laird that he was going beyond the law in this persecution. So John and I prepared to go.

Our three-year-old girlie would be left behind in Yungping in the charge of our lady colleagues, one of whom was a nurse. She would receive every care, and we planned to be gone only a month. But it tore my mother heart to pieces despite full confidence in my fellow workers. I walked out of Yungping weeping. You see, I was a "softy."

Mountain travel with my strong, young, capable hubby, then only twenty-eight years old, was like another honeymoon.

We took a route which led us up the valley of the

Mekong river which runs parallel to the Salween in northwestern Yunnan. At length we came to a hamlet where there was no proper inn. Every traveler stayed in the big adobe farmhouse of the wealthiest inhabitant. It was a sooty, dirty place. In fact, we dubbed it "the dirtiest inn in the world." We slept upstairs in the granary.

"Tomorrow we climb," John said, "the biggest climb you've ever had! We ought to be on the road by six o'clock if possible, and we climb all morning. But when you reach the top, oh, what a view! You can see the Salween mountains from there! Just think, Belle, tomorrow you will see Lisuland."

It had been ten years since I first heard of the Lisu tribe and felt called to minister to them. How I thrilled at the thought that tomorrow I would see that alpine land, even though from afar.

But early the next morning I awoke with diarrhea and an upset stomach.

"Belle!" John said in a pained voice. "Don't tell me we've got to stay another day in this place!"

"No!" I replied. "If I picked up one germ here by sleeping one night, I'd maybe have two by tomorrow night! We don't stop for this."

"But it's the hardest climb till we reach the Salween." John groaned. "How can you do it on an empty stomach and maybe with dysentery beginning?"

"Well, I'm sure I won't improve by an extra day in this dirty place," I argued. "Put me on my horse, and then all I have to do is to sit on it!"

And so we began. Up and up, back and forth as the trail zigzagged upward. About ten in the morning we came to an abandoned tribal hut.

"Here," John said, "let me make you a cup of cocoa. Do you think you could keep it down?"

I was chilled and faint and glad for a moments' rest from clinging to the animal. Glad for the warmth of the fire John built and glad when the hot liquid comforted my empty stomach. It stayed down. Then once more I went onto the animal's back.

The Mekong side of the mountain was heavily wooded, but it was interesting to note the different tree belts. On the lower slopes we had passed through feathery bamboo, which creaks loudly as the wind stirs its long tubular stems. Then tall pine trees with whispering tops awed us by their height. Still further up the trees were even greater and older, but so hung with vines, mosses, and ferns that I could not identify their kind. From the great branches the vines fell in loops and festoons perhaps twenty to fifty feet in tangled length.

The sun hardly penetrated now, and it was getting colder. My promise to sit on the horse was not so easy to keep. Chilled, stiff and weak, I felt my head begin to go round and had to pray for concentration to hold on. John watched me anxiously, cheering me by assurances that the top was not far off now.

Finally, with a lunge, my animal pulled himself up over a rocky ledge and stood trembling with relief on a level space—the top of the world! So it looked and felt.

The sun drenched us with a welcome warmth. I was surprised to see that the other side of our mountain was as shorn of tall timber as the Mekong side was shaggy with it. Scrub oak or rhododendron bushes covered its steep sides but did not obscure the scenery. Far, far below us, like a doll's house, a large farm caught our attention.

"See, Belle!" said jubilant John, "Down there is a big house where we can cook dinner. Keep your courage up. But look!" pointing to the far distance where dark purple peaks undulated along the horizon. "That is Lisuland! Those are the mountains of the Salween gorge. Tomorrow night we ought to be there."

It was a most beautiful panorama and we were tempted to stay and look, but it was already noon and we had no place to cook food until we reached that farmhouse far, far below us. With a last longing glance, we began the descent.

It was three in the afternoon before I had my first real meal that day. Luckily this trouble of the morning seemed to have quieted down during my fast.

Sunshine and only three o'clock in the afternoon—it was too much for youthful energy. John had been talking to our Chinese farmer-host. "Say, Belle, you're not going to sleep here, are you? Why, we are not even down the mountain! I've been asking and they say Old Nest, the next village, isn't far away, only about four li after you get down this hill. Let's go on and sleep there! It is a full day from there to the Salween. If we sleep here we won't make the Salween tomorrow."

Now John had misunderstood the garbled Chinese dialect of our host, who was not of pure Chinese blood. John thought he had said "three or four li" when he really said "thirty li!"—the same sort of thing that had happened when we first went to Tali.

If it had been three or four li, a little more than a mile, we would have been there in an hour or so. That is why I readily consented to leave the large comfortable farmhouse and set out for the village of Old Nest.

Once we had fully descended the mountain we found ourselves in the bottom of a deep ravine, winding our way over and around rocks, a noisy stream beside us and no sign of human habitation anywhere. At the end of two hours we were still in the depths of that rocky channel, daylight was fading, and a miserable rain had begun to fall steadily.

I had packed my raincoat somewhere in our loads, so it was not long before I was soaked, with the rain streaming off my sun helmet. John walked while I rode the animal. Still no sign of Old Nest—or any kind of a nest! It was then six o'clock by my watch.

"Belle, I pity you," said repentant Johnny. "Wouldn't you be better off if you were walking here with me? At least your blood would be circulating."

"I'm too exhausted to walk, dear. Sorry. You're right; I'm cold and stiff and faint. Where is Old Nest?"

"I must have misunderstood him, Belle. I'm so sorry. He must have said *san-shih* instead of *san si*. You know how these half-tribal fellows often pronounce it like that. But it has got to be soon. Even thirty li has to end some time!"

Perhaps it was seven o'clock when we finally climbed a hill and arrived at the sprawling village. John led me to a big adobe house that looked prosperous, explained our situation to the owner, and with true Chinese hospitality they invited us in. A huge wood fire soon blazed on their hearth, and I luxuriated in its warmth while my clothing dried out. A cup of hot tea was soon urged upon me, then hot sugar water with chopped walnuts in it, and a delicious Chinese meal was prepared. In two hours I felt like a different person.

I was the first white woman these people had seen, and the farmhouse was soon crowded with Chinese women and men looking at me and asking questions. John took the opportunity to preach the gospel to them.

Chapter Thirteen
A Glimpse of Storybook Land

THE NEXT MORNING we were up before daylight and on the road with the first beams of the rising sun. Traveling was hot and tedious. It would have been very hard if the vision seen on the mountaintop had not encouraged our hearts. This dusty tortuous way was leading to the Salween. It had an end! This is what our vision whispered. Our feet stumbled over the rocky path, but our hearts followed the vision.

At nighttime we arrived where the vision had promised, on the bank of the Salween.

The entrance to that part of Lisuland, which was to be our home for so many years, is guarded by a little market town where three feudal lords have their Yamen (official residence). It is named Luku, which translated means Six Treasuries. We were entertained by one of these lords, who took us through his castle and showed us how he had fortified it. That night after supper John whispered to me to go with him for a walk out on the mountainside. As night fell, the mountains of the opposite bank of the Salween became jet black towers. Turreted peaks pierced a dark sky spangled with brilliant stars. I was enthralled. "Storybook land!" I gasped. But soon the somber shadows of the opposite bank of mountains were broken with golden dancing spots of light.

"See that?" John whispered. "Those are Lisu fires! Lisu villages. Belle, dear, you are in Lisuland!"

I can never forget the thrill that went through me.

"My sheep wandered through all the mountains, and upon every high hill: yea, my flock was scattered upon all the face of the earth, and none did search or seek after them. My flock became meat to every beast of the field, because there was no shepherd" (Ezekiel 34:6, 8).

I was looking upon the fires of our Lord's "other sheep." "Other sheep I have, which are not of this fold: them also I must bring" (John 10:16). For unknown centuries they had been forgotten and left prey to every beast of the field, every demon of the devil's host. But now we had come as under-shepherds. Our joy and fellowship with the Great Shepherd at that moment is too sacred to describe, but it was one of life's great moments.

The next day brought a series of mountain climbs. By noon we were at a height two thousand feet above the Salween. John pointed to our afternoon road. "We drop down here," he said, "cross the stream at the bottom, climb that set of hairpin turns till level in height with where we are now, go around the brow of that hill and there is Pine Mountain Village and Leila Cooke."

I looked at the wild, chaotic pile of mountains, remembered the many days' journey between here and Chinese civilization from which we had come, heard in memory Mr. Fraser say, "She has not seen another white face for months," and my heart sat at Leila Cooke's feet.

We had wonderful fellowship together. The second day after our arrival, Mark of Goomoo with his two comrades and his challenging life story arrived. This story is told in *Nests Above the Abyss*.

By the third or fourth morning John was feeling the

need of exercise. "I think I'll just go out and help those fellows work the garden," he said to me, disappearing through the door. Leila Cooke and I were inside, busy about something, when suddenly we heard laughter, then peals of laughter, then gales of it. Leila got up, went to the door, and looked out.

"Well," she exclaimed, "I was told there was a second side to John Kuhn that few people got to see, but I didn't believe it. Now I know."

I went and looked over her shoulder. Two Lisu boys had been hoeing the rough mountainside preparatory to planting a garden. Now they were rolling on the ground holding their sides with laughter. John, who could not yet speak Lisu, so could not yet talk to them, had taken the hoe. They had looked astonished, but yielded the implement at his request. Solemnly he raised it, gave it a mighty whirl, and brought it down heavily, just missing the clod of earth aimed at. At first their laughter was covert, but when his pantomime made it obvious that he was just clowning for their benefit, their delight knew no bounds. From that day he became Big Brother, beloved and adored.

Leila Cooke was with us only long enough to explain the persecution the church was undergoing because they refused to plant opium. Then she left us to rejoin her husband who was in the Luda district, six days' journey to the north. Moses, a tribesman who spoke Chinese, was our interpreter.

Before she departed, Leila Cooke said to me, as if it were a casual matter, "Oh, by the way, Moses' wife is expecting, you know. I promised to help her. But if the baby comes before I return, you'll have to be in charge, I suppose."

"Oh!" I cried, aghast. "I couldn't! I've never seen such a thing, and I've had no training, and..."

"I haven't had training either," she replied, but there

is nobody else to help her! A Lisu woman might be obtained, but they are not clean, you know. You and I at least understand hygiene. As for not having seen a birth—you've had a baby yourself, haven't you?"

"Yes," I gasped. "But I—er—wasn't taking note of the procedure."

"Well, there are some books on obstetrics in the lower shelf," Leila said, indicating her bookcase. "And to comfort you—none of her other babies have lived. They were all stillborn. So if this one is also, you need not feel it was your fault. But I wish for Moses' sake this one could live. He would so love to have a child.... Well, goodbye. We'll pray for one another!" And off she went.

I cannot describe my feelings. Remember, I am a "softy." The very idea of being responsible for a birth gave me cold chills. I seized the obstetric books. They were full of incidents of abnormal cases. The more I read, the more nightmares I got! And it was dear Moses' wife and baby!

I had met Moses before and been deeply impressed. His breadth of brow betokened the unusual intellect he possessed, but he was so humble and modest, always shrinking into the background. I had come to love him dearly in the Lord. There was an atmosphere of rest about him, the serene peace of a life abandoned to the Lord and governed by Him. Yet he was a born leader of men. When he conducted the singing in church, there was a grace of movement and a power to inspire that I have seldom seen equaled.

Mrs. Cooke had told me how the white people in Shanghai had been thrilled with him and wanted to give him gifts, white cambric shirts among other things. "We feared that he might be spoiled before he got back to these rough hills," she continued. "But to our relief he went right into native homespun clothes, and we've never seen a sign of those cambric shirts. I've sometimes wondered what he has done with them."

A few days after she left us, there was a baptismal service at Pine Mountain. Moses, as native pastor, officiated. When he went down into the pool, he stood a moment and rolled up his sleeves. There under the navy blue homespun was a fine cambric cuff. Hastily he turned it back up and under. But I had seen it. He was wearing his Western finery, but where it would not show, and his poorer Lisu brethren would never be moved to envy by it.

Do you wonder why we loved Moses? And was I to be the one, by bungling ignorance, to cost him another child? The thought did not help to steady my nerves. Vainly, I hoped the birth would be postponed until Mrs. Cooke got back.

She had been gone perhaps ten days when Moses came to me. "Big Sister," he said, "Grace is having a stomach ache. Would you kindly come and see her?"

Quickly I went up to their shanty which stood on the slope just above ours. His wife Grace was crouched in the far corner of the room. She looked like a wild animal cornered by the inescapable, and she would obey no advice of mine! I gave all the medical counsel which had been given to me. She would act on none of it. She would not even talk with me.

"Well, we will get things sterilized and arranged, Moses," I said, my heart beating quickly. "I have studied the medical books, and we must prepare..." I named off the items. "Also, we think the baby does better if it sleeps by itself." I added this doubtfully, for I knew the Lisu did not agree with us in this.

"I would like my baby brought up like your babies," he said quickly. "Would this basket do for a baby bed?"

It was just right. With great joy, I got some materials Leila Cooke had left at my disposal, and we fixed the basket up very prettily. Moses, usually so calm and deliberate, was obviously stirred and excited. All day we waited and nothing happened. I went to bed with my clothes on, expecting an early call. None came. Grace was still where I first saw her. She would not get up, she would not walk or exercise. She just crouched in the corner.

As the day progressed, Moses got anxious. I could see it in his eyes. My eyes were nearly inflamed from poring over the medical books! They gave instructions for preparation, and advice on reception and after birth care, but not a word on what to do to induce labor.

By late afternoon, the concern in Moses' eyes haunted me. He never lost his slow serene movements, but his eyes belied that calm behavior. "Isn't there a medicine you can give her to speed it up, Ma-ma?" he asked.

I had prayed until I was nearly exhausted. John did not know any more than I did about what to do. But from somewhere in the past I thought I remembered somebody saying something about using quinine. "There is a medicine I think I heard once that someone advised. But oh, Moses, I can't be sure! No book tells me either. If it is the wrong medicine, it might kill her! And I don't know the dosage."

"I'm willing to try it," the poor fellow said, his eyes pleading for help.

"Oh, Moses, you trust me too much. I'm not sure I heard it rightly." I was in an agony of doubt. "I tell you, let us pray about it. You go back and pray, and I will stay here and pray. After ten minutes come back and we'll see how the Lord has led us."

How I pleaded that God would not let me make a mistake! Gradually the conviction came that I should try quinine in small doses. When Moses returned I asked him, "What do you think?"

"I think we should try that medicine, Ma-ma."

"I feel the same. All right, here it is. Now Moses, we are going to give her one two-grain pill every half-hour. You watch carefully. If you see any new development call me immediately." With that, for the second night I lay down in my clothes.

It was not yet midnight when a knock came at our door. I was up in a moment.

It was Moses. "Please come, Ma-ma."

I don't know how I got up that dark mountainside. I was shaking from head to foot. Had I killed her? She was lying down this time, and I turned my flashlight upon her. In another moment a little one was in our hands.

"It's dead," Moses said mournfully.

Suddenly, a piercing wail rent the air! God uses the foolish things of the earth veritably and had been merciful to this inexperienced "nurse." A lovely baby girl, whom they named Esther, was soon clean and rosy, daintily wrapped up in her wee bed, sleeping peacefully.

For the first and only time I saw Moses excited. His eyes shone like stars for joy. He ministered to the baby much more than her mother, and with such a loving tenderness and lingering over her, that it brought tears to my eyes. No sleep for him. Joy was his food and drink. He spent the hours while baby slept writing letters to all his friends and relatives. He just wanted to tell everybody that this baby had lived.

"Do you have any tinned milk, Ma-ma?" he asked. "I'd like to buy some. Baby Esther's mother cannot feed our child."

I stared at him a moment, then pulled my face straight. "I will gladly sell you milk, Moses," I said, "but it is usual for the mother not to start feeding the baby until the third day."

Oh, what a relief! Once more life was a joy, and he

turned round to speed back to his young madonna with this wonderful news.

Baby Esther grew chubby and strong. She was not yet a month old, however, before a runner came in from Allyn Cooke in the north. It contained a message something like this: "If Moses' baby has been born, please ask him to come up and help us here for three months. The work is spreading so—we need him."

"Oh," I cried to John, "how cruel to ask Moses to leave just now! Three months? Why, he will miss all the first baby awakenings, the first smile, the first laugh. Oh, I can't deliver this message."

But as it turned out, I was the one who had to do it, after all. We were standing in the main room of our shanty. Through the open door the beautiful snow-clad peaks of the opposite bank of the Salween jutted up into the blue, blue sky. As I delivered the message, Moses gave me one startled look, then turned and gazed at those steadfast sparkling peaks. Obviously he was speaking in his heart with his Lord. As I watched, his face cleared and was suffused with peace.

Turning to me he said quietly, "I will go if the Lord wants me to go." It had been but a short struggle. The one big "yes" of utter consecration had been said some years before, so that further surrender of each new gift or joy from Him did not consume much time or wrestling.

I felt I was standing on holy ground and prayed within my heart, "Lord, this is just one Lisu. If his race can produce such devotion, please take my life and use it in teaching them of You."

Chapter Fourteen
A Parting That Did Not Part

THE MONTH WE HAD PROMISED TO STAY soon drew to its close. But the opium persecution affair was not yet settled. The Lisu church desired that John stay on for a few more weeks.

He wanted to stay on, too, but I had promised the girls I would be back in about a month. It was already past that, and there was no way to telegraph them of delay. Neither could we tell when the opium business would be settled. As a matter of fact, John would not get back until June. So I felt I must return to Yungping and relieve the young missionaries of my work so they could pursue their studies.

It was decided that Ma Fu-yin go with me. He was an attractive Christian Chinese lad of about twenty who had come with us. He consented happily to be my escort back.

John thought there was a shorter route than the one via Old Nest village, but I would still have to cross the mountains. Few used that road, and I believe I am the only white woman who has ever been over it. It crossed directly to the Mekong valley. Chinese market towns dot that road, so it was easy to get food and lodging. I rode Jasper, a wily old mule lent to us by Mr. Fraser.

John and I will never forget the parting. My heart was torn between husband and child. I did not like to leave John, although our Lisu friends would feed him well and care for him. At the same time I had never before been separated from Kathy, and I could hardly wait to get back to her. John did not like to see me go either, so he decided to ride with me to the top of Place-of-Action mountain, which he reckoned would be about half way along my first day's journey.

The scenery was indescribably gorgeous. Higher up the mountain than Place-of-Action village was the village of Golden Bamboo, where we had many Christians, so we had slept there the night before and climbed from there. The road went hairpinning back and forth, back and forth, each rise in altitude giving a farther glimpse of mountain peaks behind the great summits which banked the canyon. I felt we were climbing to the top of the world. Mountaintops like the waves of the sea spread out in all directions, but the sea troughs were abysses of great depth. My heart trembled even as it thrilled.

Then the path left the banks of the Salween and began to travel into one of the tributary rivers—but it still ascended. It was a mere cow path, which necessitated our going single file. At one place we skirted a great rocky knoll and jutted out over nothing! I closed my eyes lest the drop at the side of the path should unsteady me. It would be a fearful plunge over that edge!

Till almost noon we rode. Then the path seemed to have reached the top of the range and looked level far on ahead. John reined in his horse. "Well, Belle, I guess we part here," he said.

A lump was in my throat. I must go on alone now and leave him alone.

When I have to face a separation which is painful, I like to get it over quickly. So when John called Ma Fu-yin and the Lisu carriers together for a parting prayer, I was hoping he would make it short! Not so Johnny. His disposition is quite different. Propriety is very important to him, and to hurry through such a separation is a shallow performance not worthy of a real Christian. So after a lengthy prayer he raised his voice and began to sing,

God be with you till we meet again,
By His counsels guide, uphold you,
With His sheep securely fold you,
God be with you...

Singing is just the last straw to me emotionally. The camel's back breaks every time. So when he plaintively continued, "Till we me-ee-et—Till we me-et, Till we meet at Jesus' feet," visions of all the awful things that might happen to dear Hubby in that canyon before I saw him again harrowed me until I felt I could not stand it.

But John inexorably went on, "Till we me-ee..."

I opened my eyes. "Please stop it," I was going to say, when I caught sight of a tail whisking around the corner. There was another objector: Jasper had jerked his head loose from Ma Fu-yin who, with closed eyes, was valiantly trying to follow the song, with which he was not too familiar. When I saw Jasper, his hind legs and tail were waving a gay farewell. Back down over the trail we had just come raced the animal, driving in front of him John's mount also.

John never did get this "me-ee-et" finished. I screamed, and Ma Fu-yin, feeling a jerk on his hand, came back to earth, picked up his heels, and started off in chase of Jasper and the other horse!

This was a delightful game to the mule. It was downhill the whole way, and such a narrow road that Ma Fu-yin could find no shortcut to steer him off! It was also such an untraveled road that there was nobody at all to stop him en route. Jasper and the horse raced gaily around sharp corners, Ma Fu-yin after them, legs and arms flying like a windmill.

Out of sight of his pursuer Jasper would stop to nibble the delicious green grasses richly banking the wild path. As the human windmill turned the corner and came into view, off went the two animals again.

Left horseless on that high trail, we waited for a while, then decided to walk together back down the trail, hoping against hope to meet Ma Fu-yin with a subdued and repentant Jasper in tow. No such good fortune! Hour after hour we plodded on foot back over the way we had ridden. Finally we came again to the banks of the Salween. Far down, almost to Golden Bamboo Village we beheld Ma Fu-yin with Jasper in tow at last.

But it was now too late in the day to proceed. That night we slept in the same place from which we had left that morning.

"Now don't you think it is the Lord trying to persuade you to stay with me?" suggested Hubby hopefully the next morning.

"No," said his stubborn spouse. "I think it is a warning to you not to indulge in such long drawn-out partings!"

This time John decided not to escort me, but he took a seat on a big stone by the side of the road. As our party ascended back and forth over the hairpin turns, he became smaller and smaller, until he looked the size of a pin head, still waving his handkerchief.

The rest of the day's journey was lonely but grand. At the very top of the range we came upon a little sun-kissed meadow where a sparkling clean brook gurgled, a wonderful place for a camp. But we pressed on. Dusk was falling before we even began to descend. Finally I got off the weary mule and stumbled down the mountainside with only pale moonlight to show the trail. We stopped for the night at the first village.

The next day's journey was most pleasant. The road wound through rice fields beginning to show their emerald green, and often by the banks of the blue Mekong river.

Late that afternoon we came to a small market town beside the first bridge we had seen. Here there was a small inn with a stable in the inner courtyard. Ma Fu-yin came to me. "Szu-mu," he said, "I don't think that stable will keep this mule inside. He is devilish wise, you know. I've never met such an animal, and I have misgivings about what he'll do tonight."

The owner of the place seemed to be a woman. "Da-ma" (great mother), I said to her, "Haven't you a door for that stable? I fear our mule will get out if you haven't."

"Get out of my stable? Nonsense!" she said. "It has bars that are put across. Animals stay there all the time—nothing ever gets out."

"But our mule is old and wise. I fear those bars won't hold him. Can't you help us make it more secure?"

"No need, no need," she said confidently. "I'll guarantee he'll not get out if you put the bars down."

About three o'clock the next morning I was awakened by a most fearful racket downstairs. An excited voice was swearing in a high-pitched tone. Something big was being whacked! It sounded like an elephant in a china shop.

Suddenly a shrill neigh awoke my suspicions. I sat up in bed and called out, "Ma Fu-yin!"

Soon his slender form appeared in my doorway. He was shaking with suppressed laughter. Chinese oaths and execrations continued, mingled with whacks, from below.

"It was Jasper!" whispered Ma Fu-yin. "During the

night he lifted the stable bars off with his nose, strode out into the courtyard, smelled Da-ma's big pan of bean curd which she had made to sell on the market today. He went into her kitchen and had eaten about half of it before she woke up and found him!"

It was an irate innkeeper who said goodbye to us after breakfast.

Naughty as Jasper was, I never forgot that the old mule did me one great favor. Thereafter, whenever a painful and prolonged parting was in prospect I had only to say pleadingly, "John, please! Remember Jasper!"

CHAPTER FIFTEEN
The Thing with the Stuff in It

IT WAS DECEMBER OF 1934 before we were finally able to move into Lisuland as a family. It was quite an undertaking. Almost the only vegetable that could be purchased at Pine Mountain was corn. Sometimes a salt merchant came around, rice could be bought, and chickens were frequently obtainable. We traded medicine for eggs—an egg for a pill—not evaluating the size of the pill or the age the egg! But flour, sugar, tinned milk, and tinned goods we must bring in. Clothes and bedding must also be packed for horse loads, as well as kerosene for light, tools for building, books and medicine.

The money used in the canyon was silver, which weighed heavily if you were taking in enough for several months' living expenses. We would need to hire carriers, also servants, since water had to be carried from well to house. The nearest mailbox was a day's journey away. All in all, we found ourselves with eleven pack horses.

John decided that the easiest route for pack animals was via Old Nest village. So we started out. The weather was beautiful—clear blue skies with golden sunshine and just enough nip in the air to stimulate exercise and appetite.

Since Kathryn was with us, she and I rode in a sedan chair while John rode Jasper. Where it was too steep for the porters to carry baby and me together, I got out and rode the mule while John walked.

It was pleasant traveling up the beautiful Mekong valley, but eventually, of course, we came to "The Dirtiest Inn in the World." We had a merry time in that sooty farmhouse. Cooped up all day long in the chair, Kathryn was all activity as soon as we got out. She was three years old and into everything. Much can be washed off with cold water, but not soot! To get hot water, we had to heat it in a grimy pot over an open wood fire on the floor or in the courtyard. Our patience was tried to the breaking point. We longed for nightfall in order to put Kathryn to bed. We tried to get everything packed up and breakfast cooked before we woke Kathryn in the morning, so that she would not look like a chimney sweep by the time we started.

At length we were ready. Loads were lined up waiting to have the horses led under them. We had finished breakfast and I had saved some warm water to give Kathryn a last hand wash before I put her in the chair.

For myself, I despaired of ever starting out clean. The place was such a junk shop and the low ceilings so festooned with sooty cobwebs, I had only to turn round and something was sure to brush a black mark against my cheek, skirt or my hands. Unknown to me, John had found it as irritating as I had. He had prepared some hot water in a different room and made up his mind to have a wash just before setting out.

Muleteers, chair porters, Kathryn and I were all ready to leave. But where was John? We usually had prayer together before setting out. "John," I called. "Hurry up! We're all waiting for you."

No answer. Where could he be? I was about to call again when he emerged from a side room beaming with amiability. "See, Belle," he said, glowing with success, and holding out two spotless palms for my admiration. "At least I'm clean when I leave."

"What on earth!" He had turned over his newly washed hands and there, behold, a black streak of soot across the back of one! He must have brushed against something as he came out the door! "Would you look at that!" he said, disgusted. "What a place! Well I'll..." and he began peering into this load and that one. "Belle, where is the thing with the stuff in it?"

I stood, knitting my brow, trying to think what he meant.

But he interpreted my silence as non-cooperation. "Where's that thing with the stuff in it?" he shot at me again.

The muleteers could not understand English, but they knew that something concerning the loads had displeased their sunny-tempered master and had a feeling it would be wise to appear industrious at this moment. So they began pulling at ropes and poking at the horses with an anxious manner.

Only I stood there, appearing idle. In reality I was scurrying around mentally, trying to guess what John was hunting for.

"Belle!" he protested. "Why don't you help a fellow? You stand there gaping—where's that thing with the stuff in it?"

My indignation broke. "I defy anyone in this universe to help you, John Kuhn, when you use such ambiguous language. A thing with the stuff in it? Why, everywhere I look," indicating the eleven horse loads, "everywhere I look there are things with stuff in them!"

But my retort was lost. He was half buried in the depths of one basket from which he emerged at last, smiling and calm, holding up a tube of hand cream. "Don't get excited, dear," he said, soothingly, "I just thought this would take the soot mark off. I'm ready now."

The muleteers, seeing that the sun was shining again, straightened up with relief and began to call the animals forward. And John led us in prayer for protection on the road that day.

As we began to climb a particularly difficult and arduous part of the ascent I began to picture to John the scene of the morning, mimicking his question until its unreasonableness dawned upon him. He began to laugh—until he could hardly climb. It has become another of our family jokes. In fact, for twelve years now it has helped us over the small crises of life when something quickly needed is difficult to lay hands on. If one of us roars, "The thing with the stuff in it?" then in the midst of subsequent laughter a more accurate description speedily follows.

Chapter Sixteen
Furlough without Baggage (1936)

SIXTEEN MONTHS OF HAPPY WORK in Lisuland followed. These included the building of our shanty, "Home of Grace." John always hoped he would not be asked to build a house on the mission field, but when it fell to his lot, he built it so strong that it stood for some twenty years—until the Communists tore it down.

Now it was time for our first furlough. We sailed from Shanghai on the *President McKinley* and had the joy of fellowship with a missionary family in the cabin next to us. The wife and I had sailed to China together as single missionaries, and as true CIMers we had prayer together daily in our cabin.

On one of these occasions, we had just finished and were in the act of getting off our knees. A fellow passenger, dashing merrily down the corridor, mistook our cabin for his own and barged in. The poor man was not only surprised, he was petrified! When he arrived so suddenly in our midst, we were neither on our knees, nor as yet upright. We were halfway up, groping in the air. He looked as if he thought he had landed in a cell of an insane asylum, and his face so clearly revealed his thoughts that we fell back in our chairs, convulsed with laughter.

In those days, ocean liners held a "Hard Time Party" once during the voyage. One day it was announced for the evening meal. The steward informed us that we would not be served dinner unless we appeared in costume. He looked at the two CIM missionary families as he said this, possibly thinking that people who had a prayer meeting every day would be too long faced for fun making. We did not undeceive him.

It was John's costume I remember best. He dressed as a bold pirate in a sleeveless waistcoat and a pair of shorts with a gay sash around the middle. Into this was stuck a hunting knife. The red bandanna tied round his head was splashed with mercurochrome, and he blackened hollows under his eyes with burnt cork. The cork also produced streaks of soot on his cheeks, shoulders and legs. The mercurochrome supplied more gory-looking gashes for neck and limbs. Under the bandanna, his hair was combed down over his eyes. Being big, muscular and hairy, he was a fearsome sight.

I had pulled my hair back tight from my face and did it up in a teapot handle, an imitation of Maggie Jiggs. With long skirts to the floor, I looked the part.

We sailed together into the dining room, a trifle late, and solemnly faced the steward. He had prided himself on being able to identify everybody. But as we stood there, John scowling in good pirate fashion, and I looking down the length of my nose at him, the steward was dumbfounded. Giggles came from those already seated. He looked around to see who was yet missing to help him catch a clue, but several seats were vacant. He could not guess our identity for the life of him. Finally he had to ask who we were!

As we passed between tables, one of the men called out, "You take first prize, sir!" When it got noised about that the ferocious pirate was the supposedly long-faced missionary, one of the other male guests got up and came to John. "Congratulations!" he said. "You're a good sport."

If the rest of the evening had been games and good fun, it would have been a happy evening. But when dinner was over, drinking began. That soon drove us to our cabin, so we were not present when the prizes were awarded.

Our ship did not dock at Vancouver, where my father and brother lived. The destination was Seattle. We had to disembark at Victoria and take a coastal steamer from there to Vancouver. John was given baggage tickets to see to the transfer of our luggage from the one ship to the other. We were not prepared, however, for the wonderful reception that the mission friends in Victoria gave us. Since the local boat did not leave immediately, they had planned a trip for us to Buchard's Sunken Gardens. Just to see homeland shores was thrilling enough, but the excitement of meeting everybody eclipsed everything else.

It was only after the ship to Vancouver was actually pulling out of Victoria harbor that John suddenly clapped his hands on his pocket. With chagrin, he pulled out the baggage tickets and held them up to me. "Belle, look! I completely forgot about them!"

"Oh, John!" That meant we had nothing but what we had on—not even an overnight case!

A hasty interview with the purser brought comfort. We could wire for our things to be forwarded to us on the next ship. That night, amid much laughter, our friends brought us night clothes to sleep in.

The arrival in Vancouver was memorable. My father and brother were at the dock, of course. But somehow, I had not expected so many of my girl friends also to be there. There they were. It was exciting to lead John up to them and make him guess from my previous descriptions just who was who. He did not make many mistakes.

Kathryn monopolized Grandpa. We had carefully

built up a story around him, telling of the peppermint candy that always hid in his pockets, and so on. We hoped she would not be strange with him, and she wasn't. In fact, she clung to him so that he could go nowhere without her.

When bedtime came, Kathryn calmly announced that she was going to sleep with Grandpa. On his side, he could refuse her nothing. We dubiously wished him a good night with his sidekick.

Their bedroom was across a short hall from ours, and the next morning early, before anyone was out of bed, we overheard the following conversation:

Grandpa: "What are you going to have for breakfast?"

Kathryn: "I don't know, but I am going to put candy in my breakfast to make it taste good. You have big ears."

Grandpa: "Well, isn't that wonderful. Haven't you big ears?"

Kathryn: "Oh no, I have little ears. But when I grow up I will have big ears—bigger than yours!"

Grandpa coughed.

Kathryn: "When you cough you should cover your mouth with your hand like this—or it might get on me!"

And so began Grandpa's education.

A few days later, our trunks appeared. All the way from Lisuland to Vancouver, we had experienced the covering of His hand, keeping bad things from "getting on" his children.

CHAPTER SEVENTEEN
Working the Thing That is Good

WE WERE IN VANCOUVER for about three weeks, then crossed into the United States to attend The Firs Bible and Missionary Conference at Bellingham, Washington. This was the conference where I had first offered my life for foreign service, and I wanted my friends there to get to know John.

This year the chief speakers were Dr. Lewis Sperry Chafer, Mr. L. E. Maxwell of Prairie Bible Institute, Dr. John G. Mitchell, and Miss Frances Brook. All four left a permanent imprint on our lives.

Among the many dear saints of the Lord who attended that conference were Mr. and Mrs. Eastman. They lived on Orcas Island in Puget Sound, a favorite summer resort. There they had built a few summer cottages as an investment. One of these they had dedicated to the Lord to be loaned to missionaries who needed rest. When they offered it to us, urging us to come at the end of the conference, we promised to pray about it.

I was still underweight, due to a hard bout of sickness before furlough. I was also highly strung and worn after eight years of service on the field. I needed to quietly get away from even the dear excitement of visiting old friends. John, who takes life more calmly, was in no such need. He liked to be on the go, loved to visit, did not require a full night's sleep, and could even lengthen the day until midnight. Yet we did not like to separate—that was not any fun either. It was obvious that I must get where I could sleep and relax, so that August saw us established in a couple of rooms over a garage in Orcas Island. A nearby cabin in the woods housed Grandpa Miller, who could not bear to be parted from us.

It proved to be a beautiful little island with a permanent farming community. In fact, right behind us was a small farm where a middle-aged couple had built a two-roomed cabin. As the sale of produce from their farm brought in sufficient money, they were adding a third room about the time of our arrival.

I was ordered to sleep late every morning to try to build up physically. But healthy John found time hanging heavy on his hands. Grandpa liked to fish, but that did not solve John's need for exercise. Finally one morning he announced, "There is an old man next door roofing a side wing of his cabin. He seems to be all alone, and I wonder if he wouldn't like help. I'm going to offer. I just must get some physical work, or I'll get fat and lazy. Come on, Grandpa, you're good for a few shingles and nails, aren't you?"

Grandpa, who thought the world of his son-in-law, could not deny it. That morning saw the short fat figure and the tall muscular one approach the new wing where our neighbor was perched on the rafters, nails in his mouth, shingles and hammer in his hands.

"Hi there!" John called out. "Want any help? We'd be glad to come up and assist you!"

The farmer, known as Grandpa Loomis, peered over the edge and looked down on the smiling young face. "Oh-a," he began in embarrassment, "We're just building ourselves. It doesn't matter if it goes slow. I just do a little each day as I can and ..."

It was Grandpa Miller who caught on first. "Oh, we

don't want wages," he called back. "Son here has nothing to do and wants some exercise, that's all."

Grandpa Loomis could not believe his ears. A laborer without wages! That was worth investigating. "Just a moment," he called. "I'm coming down. I don't hear too good any more."

A few seconds later, around the corner of the wooden shell, he appeared. "Come on in and have a cup of coffee," he said, ushering them into the two-room shack where a portly figure in a big kitchen apron eyed them with astonishment.

"This is Grandma Loomis," he said, introducing her carelessly. "Get us some coffee, Old Girl, will you? These are the missionaries, our new neighbors. What did you say was the name?"

"Mine is John Kuhn," said the young stalwart, "and this is my wife's father. We call him Grandpa Miller. Glad to meet you, Mrs. Loomis. We were wondering if your husband would let us help him nail on that roof. You see, I need exercise. I feel myself getting flabby doing nothing. We don't want money for it, just the privilege of getting the fresh air and activity."

It was now Grandma Loomis' turn to be astonished. Her husband, who now realized he had heard correctly, beamed. "It would sure go faster, Ina," he said eagerly. "And maybe I'd even be able to get some boarding up!"

"Well, I take that as mighty kind," said dear old Grandma Loomis. "But you ought to be told that it is pretty hot up there on the roof."

"Oh, that's okay," John said. "A good sweat is healthy. How about getting to work now? Can you find an extra hammer, do you think?"

So it came about that, lying on my bed in the flat, I could hear, along with the call of sea birds, the rat-a-tat-tat of two or three hammers on the Loomis' roof behind us.

Five-year-old Kathryn was, of course, with the working contingent. She played house with broken shingles and wandered with Grandma Loomis through her vegetable garden and was content.

The old couple were simply thrilled with their wageless laborers. They kept up a steady stream of gifts from their garden. Squash, beans, cucumbers—whatever they had—found its way to our kitchen.

More than that, when John went to the corner grocery to buy some coffee, the proprietor beamed at him. "Aren't you the missionary who is working for Grandpa Loomis? We hear you're going to preach for Mr. Eastman Sunday night. Well, we're coming. Guess you'll have a pretty good crowd! Your reputation has sort of got around the island. A missionary working like that and for nothing, you know. Everybody is talking about it."

So the heart of the island opened to us. We were invited to this farmstead and that. And we formed friendships that lasted for years. In fact, I believe that on Orcas Island there are some who still pray for the Kuhn family and the Lisu tribe.

Once again, we found that the Lord's way is the happy way. John's surrender for my sake was blessed and brought joy and happiness to many more beside himself.

Chapter Eighteen
Home Town

With strength renewed we left the Pacific northwest for a visit to Daddy's home town, Manheim, Pennsylvania. After the train sped across the three thousand intervening miles, we finally saw the rolling farmlands that gave us the signal that we were nearing our station, Lancaster. We all got excited.

It had been ten years since John had sailed for China and this was his first return home. Although I had visited his sister at one time, this was my first visit as a member of the family.

Who would be at the station to meet us? John's parents were both dead, but he had two half-brothers, Bill and Jim, who still lived there with Aunt Annie and Uncle Anton. Then there was John's "spiritual mother," Mrs. John Kready. John's own mother had died when he was three years old, and dear Mrs. Kready had taken him on her heart to pray him into the Kingdom. Later she stood behind him in prayer as he went down to God's front line of battle in China. Already Mother Kready's letters and spiritual premonitions of our needs had made a great impression on me. Would she be at the station?

I was also most anxious to meet a certain young bookkeeper named Mary Zimmerman. While we were still in China, I had felt I should write once a month to people who really prayed for the work. But it would cost too much to post a monthly letter to many people directly from China. So I had prayed, "Lord, if you want this letter multiplied you will have to find a way. About six months or a year later, a request came from Mary, whom I had never heard of before. She asked permission to duplicate our monthly prayer letters and include them in a little periodical she compiled each month. It was called *The Triangle*. At that time, it only went to about one hundred people; but still that meant one hundred to pray for the Lisu! I was very grateful. Would Mary be at the station to meet us?

There were others, too, of whom John had spoken often and whose faces I had seen only in snapshots. Would I recognize them?

The train was pulling to a stop. We must not forget our baggage a second time. In another minute we were on the platform, surrounded by people! I could hear John's voice joyously naming them. "Aunt Annie! Brother Bill! Brother Jim! Mother Kready!"

Then almost immediately a plump young woman in a Mennonite cap edged forward. "I'm Mary Zimmerman," she said. "Could you speak for me at a meeting on the eighteenth?"

I gasped. How often I have chuckled over that first meeting with Mary! She had only her noon hour for time off, of course, and she has the remarkable ability to make every moment count, an ability which has enabled her to do the work of several people. She wanted me to speak to her prayer group, knowing it would do much for me as well as for them. "The Lancaster Prayer Group" has been our family name for them for years, and what they contributed to the progress of the work in their quiet, hidden ministries we do not yet fully know.

My head was going round with all the excitement.

"Why yes, I'd be glad to speak," I managed to reply.

"Good. I'll *leave* you know the details and arrange transportation for you later," she added, with that perfect attention to business detail which blesses her friends. It was also my introduction to the quaint Pennsylvania Dutch way of putting things. Their dialect has simply translated German idiom into English. For example, "Walk the street down and turn the corner up." It was just part of my introduction to John's home town.

Finally, we were escorted into brother Bill's car and whirled off to Manheim. Lancaster County, with its green hills and beautifully kept farmhouses and barns, is one of the lush spots of America. John was thrilled. Looking from one side to the other, recognizing landmarks, he chatted with the relatives, sometimes trying to point out places to me.

As the car curved to the left, John called out, "Manheim Park, Belle. That is where we went for picnics and..." I caught a fleeting glimpse of a little wooded dell with swings and slides for children and picnic tables under the trees.

Then we were in the town itself. I had been brought up in the wide open spaces of western lands, and my first impression was of the houses opening right off the street and closely packed together. In the west, almost everybody had a front garden, a back yard, and side yards; each home was a unit by itself. But here they were built two together like Siamese twins. To have the doorstep opening right onto the street gave me the quaint feeling of being in medieval Germany. Everything was other-worldish, and the sight of people on the street in Mennonite costume increased the impression that I had walked into the pages of a storybook.

The car drove up to one of the double houses and

Aunt Annie called out that we were home. Everything was immaculately clean. Annie and Anton, as their nephews called them, had no children, and were of the indefatigable, industrious type. We were soon called down to supper, and I was introduced to Pennsylvania Dutch hospitality. For example, there were three or four different kinds of pie on the table at the same time.

In my innocence I offered to help with the housework. I was dubiously given the hanging up of the laundry. I had no more than a line full up when one of the family asked, horrified, "Isobel, did nobody ever teach you how to hang up clothes?" Quickly they hauled off everything I had hung up lest the neighbors discover that John's wife did not know any better than that!

No, no one had ever taught me there was an Emily Post set of rules for hanging out clothes. I had to learn from the bottom up. John's wife might do as a public speaker or even a missionary author, but as far as the practical things of life were concerned, well, it was easy to see I was not brought up in Manheim! But on the whole, they were very indulgent with me.

Manheim was then a town of about four thousand inhabitants. The Kuhn homestead, John's birthplace, now belonged to an older brother of John's father. We went around to see it and to inspect the old swimming hole at the end of the street. From there we went to the Hershey Machine and Foundry Company where John had worked for a year to earn money to start studies at Moody Bible Institute. Then off we went to see the school John had attended, and from there down Main Street, dropping in at the drug store so I could meet some distant relatives.

Mr. and Mrs. Harry Ruhl, who ran Ruhl's Drug Store, were fine Christian people. Many a present of medicine for the Lisu found its way to China from these dear ones. Lisu over many miles of hills came to know and ask for the help of a certain "pink pill" which they declared was second to none in curing stomach ache!

On down Main Street was the corner of the Square. "Here is where everybody comes on Saturday night," John explained. "People drive in from the country to do their shopping, and everywhere there is lively chatter and life bubbling with interest. Kathryn and I used to hold open-air services here when we were home from Moody. I've preached many a time at the corner there."

Near the Square was the home of a fine Christian businessman who helped John first at Moody Bible Institute and then in China. He loved the Lord Jesus Christ and his keen business mind was used in his Christian living and giving until his Home call. It was a privilege to discuss problems with him and watch "sanctified common sense" go into action.

There was one more place on the town square which demanded a visit from us: the bank. In it was deposited the cash legacy which came to John on his father's death. It was a nice little nest egg. We had recently been reading C. T. Studd's life, and it had made a real impression on us. Studd had given away his entire fortune. John was for doing the same, but I felt we should be careful not to rush into such action.

I reminded John of the need of my father, an earnest Christian and a deacon in the church, who had no compunctions about going into debt. He would even run up a charge account when he did not have sufficient income to pay for it. He was always optimistically expecting something to "turn up."

To my dear husband's credit, in accord with the challenge of 1 Timothy 5:8, the first checks drawn on his legacy wiped out my father's debt. It amounted to nearly five hundred dollars. The remainder we offered to the Lord on our knees. We rose expecting Him to tell us where it should be given.

It was a thrilling and sweet adventure to watch His finger pointing. One hundred was given to an earnest young missionary working on the border of Russia. Another hundred helped outfit a new worker for Africa. Others gifts enabled a fine Christian girl to finish at Prairie Bible Institute, sent a missionary to South America, and enabled a Manheim girl to go to Moody Bible Institute. This last young woman, from John's own home town, met and married a keen soul winner at MBI, and together they have been shining lights for the Lord in Central America for many years.

As for us, we lacked nothing. We were without a car, so friends offered to help so that we never lacked transportation. Speaking engagements piled up, and a generous friend provided my "platform clothes." Others cared for John, and still others sent Kathryn to kindergarten.

These provisions were all the more astounding because everybody in Manheim must have heard the amount Father Kuhn had left to his children. We told no one what John did with his share, not even our brothers and sisters, so our friends could not have thought we were financially pinched. It was the Lord who prompted them to care for our needs, as He had prompted us to meet the needs of His other children in other parts of the world.

"God is no man's debtor," said one of Hudson Taylor's friends to him, and we have proved it true.

As I sit back and view that small town community, removed by space and over a period of some thirty years, "the inheritance of the saints" is the most outstanding impression of that addition to my life. Gradually, I have come to see that with my husband I gained a rich portion of that great inheritance of saints.

Chapter Nineteen
The Ticklish Question

THE TIME WAS NOW APPROACHING when our daughter must enter school, and we ourselves were due to return to the field. How can the child of missionaries, especially pioneer missionaries working on a far and primitive field, get an education?

This is *the* most ticklish of all missionary problems, and feelings run deep and warm on the subject.

To keep a child alone among adults, especially one of Kathy's gregarious disposition, was a positive cruelty. The way she trembled with delight at the idea of playmates stabbed my heart. To let her continue to play with the Lisu children was also out of the question. I remembered the words of the fellow worker, a child of the mission who had warned me not to expose my child to the immoral things she might see and hear from native playmates. "I'd give anything if I could wipe out some of my childhood memories," she had said. "My parents were good missionaries, but they thought if they put the work first, God would take care of their children."

The wife of our general director had also warned me along this line shortly after I arrived in China. With tears in her eyes, she shared from her own experience. "The training of children to know the Lord is also the Lord's work," she had said.

I felt this was the voice of the Lord to me, especially as I had already felt that before God I was surely more responsible for the souls I brought into existence than for those someone else did! But The Ticklish Question had been answered only theoretically: the child's spiritual welfare must take precedence over everything else. It did not answer the question of where Kathryn should get her education.

Chefoo, the famous CIM school for missionary children, was in a beautiful and healthful spot by the seashore with all kinds of recreation available. It was staffed by missionaries whose educational qualifications were of the best. Their supreme concern was the spiritual care of their pupils.

The majority of the children saw their parents at least once a year, usually going home for a prolonged Christmas holiday. Parents in faraway pioneer places, where travel took so much time, were expected to ask the children to be sent to them only once in two years. Although this was lengthened more than once because of war, longer separations were not CIM's intent. Our own girlie was separated from us for six years at once stretch because of the Japanese war, when the Japanese interned her with her school. Though they never captured us, we were not able to get to her. She was satisfied, however, that the separation was not anything we could help.

To me the all-important thing is that the child is convinced of the unwavering love of Daddy and Mommy, convinced that nobody or nothing in the work would ever compete in their affections. If the little heart is convinced of this, it will snuggle down and gain the sense of security a child needs.

But if the parents do not write regularly, what is the child to think? Even if the child shows little interest in the parents' letters, often preferring to play, the fact that the love words have come as usual gives an unconscious satisfaction.

The child also naturally expects that her parents will make every effort possible to see her or have her home for holidays. Parents, engrossed in their work, may not realize how their child counts on this. If the parents were supremely concerned about the child, the opportunity would not be neglected, no matter how inconvenient.

If the child is assured that her parents love her only second to the Lord Himself, she can take a painfully lengthened separation and not be discouraged, her faith unshaken.

So we came to the conclusion that the CIM school was the way for us. Now came the preparation of the child's heart.

We did not spring it on Kathryn. When I told her that Chefoo School meant "lots and lots of children to play with" she clapped her hands in anticipation and joy. In every possible way, I tried to build up a love for Chefoo before she went. I think this is important. Children catch "attitudes" from their parents. If the parent is secretly rebellious and critical, the child will sense it and there is little possibility the child will fit in happily, no matter how the teachers try to help her. We prayed continually that Kathy would be happy at Chefoo School, sincerely desiring what our lips asked of God. She was.

Since Kathryn had passed her sixth birthday while on that first furlough, we faced putting her in Chefoo School as soon as we returned. But on the eve of departure, 1937, the war with Japan broke out. Chefoo waters were declared too dangerous for us.

An alternative was to take her to Yunnan and put her in our inter-mission school. Her aunt, Kathryn Kuhn Harrison, lived in Kunming, and Kathy could board with her and her husband.

So we sailed from Vancouver, having to go to Japan first, then trans-ship to Hong Kong. This took some weeks, and as war tensions relaxed, it was found that Butterfield and Swire ships were going safely between Hong Kong and Chefoo. Just at that time, the mission decided to call Miss Grace Liddell from Yunnan temporarily to fill a place on the Chefoo staff. She would be trans-shipping at Hong Kong at the same time we would, so it was planned that she escort Kathryn to Chefoo.

Therefore, on our arrival in Hong Kong, where we had expected to continue to Hanoi together as a family, I was handed a telegram before we even disembarked. It read something like this: "Liddell will escort Kathryn Kuhn to Chefoo from Hong Kong." Miss Liddell herself came out in a launch to meet us and told us gently that the ship was due to leave "three days from now."

It was a severe shock to me because I had been so unprepared for it. I had been making plans to put Kathy into the small school in Kunming, which would be so much nearer to us. After reading the telegram, I went down to our cabin to get Kathy ready. She was asleep in the top bunk, her pretty curly lashes dark against the soft pink cheeks. As I stood and gazed at her, the thought came: *You will never again have the joy of caring for her, watching her grow and develop.* I was pierced to the depths.

A little box of Bible promises lay on the bed table. I seized it and cried in my heart, *Oh God, speak to me!* I drew out Ecclesiastes 11:1, "Cast thy bread upon the waters: for thou shalt find it after many days." I felt it was His voice saying, "Cast thy child upon me. I will take good care of her and after many days thou shalt have her back again, more securely yours in heart and spirit than ever she was in mere flesh."

I cannot tell you how it comforted me. I clung to it. But because I continually dwelt on what I was losing, I was in torture. *This is the last time I give her a bath, the last time I buckle on her sandals, the last time I comb her hair!* Never can I forget the agony of those hours in Hong Kong when we said goodbye and after the ship pulled out.

Miss Liddell was everything I could have wished and more. Long before they reached Chefoo, Kathryn had learned to love her like an "own" aunt. It meant that at Chefoo, among the staff, there was one who was like a mother to her, one who was familiar and "brought familiar comforting."

As for me, John's kindness and patience is a memory for which I can never cease to bless God. For the twenty-four hours after Kathryn left, and before our own ship was due to leave, he walked the streets with me. He never seemed to weary. He just stayed with me until I was so physically exhausted I could lie down and drop into oblivion. How grateful I was, and am, for that patience and indulgence! I was wrong to get distraught, and the Lord Himself would deal with me about it. But I was quietly indulged until the time I could bear correction. As I look back on it now, I am completely satisfied with the Lord's choosing and working.

Just before the capture by the Japanese, Kathryn had a spiritual experience which prepared her to take it victoriously. Only God could have arranged that! And only He could have planned that our beloved Mrs. J. O. Fraser, with her three daughters, was interned along with Kathryn and "mothered" her during those days of scarce mail and prolonged separation from us.

Kathryn was repatriated on the second mercy trip of the Gripsholm and took notice of the preserving care of God for them on their long trip past India and South

America. The Gripsholm had a lighted cross at the top of the ship and it seemed to the twelve-year-old a symbol of the presence of Christ, leading and protecting them.

Arriving in America, she was taken into the home of George and Magdalene Sutherland of the CIM home staff in Philadelphia. She was cared for like a daughter until we could return from China ourselves. The Sutherlands were friends of ours since Moody days, and they acted as Kathryn's foster parents.

In the goodness of God to us after our second furlough, I was with Kathryn nearly two years before leaving again for another term in China. The Japanese war had left communications and travel so disrupted that women and children were not allowed back immediately. This lengthened my normal furlough span. When we left her, she was again taken into the Sutherlands' home, and during the difficult high-school years she had their love and guidance to help her.

In 1950 I was back with her. The Communists had taken over, and I had taken Danny and fled out through Burma. John stayed behind to help the church. By this time, Kathy was in Wheaton College, so we headed for Wheaton. Again the Lord prolonged my stay with her into two years. I waited a year and a half for John to be released from China. Then he needed six months' rest before our arduous pioneer work in Thailand began. God had seen to it that our girlie had her mother during the last two important college years.

So "the ticklish question" of how to educate our daughter was solved step by step as it was submitted to Him. We experienced long separations, but we also spent two years continual living together twice over.

Just before we sailed for Thailand in 1952 we saw Kathy off for the Aldrich home while she took a course in the Multnomah Bible School in Portland, Oregon.

Kathy wanted some experience of life in the business world without the shelter of a Christian home, so she accepted a teaching post at Grass Valley, Oregon. By the end of that year she knew God wanted her on the mission field. So the next time she and I met, our Kathy was an accepted candidate of the China Inland Mission. Out on the field in North Thailand she met Don Rulison, M.A. and Master of Forestry. They became engaged and later married.

As for God, his way is perfect.

What Happened After

AFTER WORLD WAR II, John Kuhn was called back to China for an important tribal survey. Once again, John and Isobel faced the challenge of their motto, *God First*. John sailed alone.

"The Lord gave us 2 Corinthians 4:12," Isobel wrote. "'So then death worketh in us, but life in you.' We felt the separation meant 'death' in the sense of breaking up our family life, but that the Lisu might gain spiritually."

In 1947 Isobel returned to Lisuland with Danny. Only a year later, Communist brigands invaded Oak Flat village where they had been staying. But by then missionaries and Bible school had moved across the river. Isobel and Danny would not leave Lisuland until March 10, 1950, trekking out over the western wall of China's border mountains into Burma. She would never return.

With China closed, the CIM began to move into new fields. The Kuhns were called to work among the tribes of North Thailand. Isobel would remain there until 1954 when cancer forced her return to the United States. God would give her three more years and her beloved John would be at her side when it came time for her real home coming (March 20, 1957). "If I was ever near heaven," John said of her last moments, "and if I ever was conscious that death has lost its sting, it was then."

"I'll be spending my time (in heaven) hanging over the ramparts greedily watching North Thailand, so that all the angels will see of me will be my heels!!! Not allowed? We'll see."

Isobel Kuhn, letter dated January 28, 1956

OTHER BOOKS BY ISOBEL KUHN

By Searching (Autobiography, Vol. 1)

An autobiography with a difference, remarkable for its honesty and frankness. It portrays Isobel's determined journey from agnosticism to faith.

In the Arena (Autobiography, Vol. 2)

"When people read this book I want them to see You, O Lord. When they find me in a perfectly hopeless situation, as so often I was, I want them to know clearly it was You who did pull me out."

Second-Mile People

Six of those who most influenced Isobel in her youth and her early years as a missionary to China.

Stones of Fire

The gripping true story of Mary, a young Lisu tribeswoman. "The stone is only a stone until its heart is broken and the air has a chance to get in."

Ascent to the Tribes

The beginnings of missionary work among a tribal people in North Thailand.

Green Leaf in Drought

The story of the escape of the last CIM missionaries from Communist China.

Nests Above the Abyss

The dramatic work of the Holy Spirit among the Lisu people of southwest China, among whom Isobel lived and worked.

Children of the Hills

Formerly *Precious Things of the Lasting Hills*, this is the story of their first encounter with the loveable Lisu people.